373 Days Afloat

(and counting)

Andrew Dalby

PublishNation, London

www.publishnation.co.uk

*This book is dedicated to
my grown up children,
Martin and Hannah.*

About the Author

Andrew Dalby is a British born musician, composer and writer. Born in North Yorkshire in 1962 he learnt to play the trumpet and after attending the Welsh College of Music and Drama in Cardiff spent twelve years as a school teacher, later becoming a self-employed musician. Amongst his many achievements he has taught scores of individuals to play musical instruments, is the founder of the Thirsk and District Royal British Legion Brass Band (which he started with a few friends in 1985) and has composed a number of works including a string quartet, a viola concerto, a Requiem Mass and many short pieces for brass band. He has two grown up children, Martin and Hannah, and now lives with his wife Claire aboard their sailing yacht "Drumlin" on the west coast of Scotland.

B-B-Q

Life is like a barbeque!
It seems to take ages to warm up,
Then nothing cooks properly,
Or gets burnt 'cos it's too hot!
Then it dies down when there's lots left to do,
And it smoulders all night,
Long after the party's over. Leaving?
A pile of ash, where once burned flames to feed hunger.

Andrew Dalby, Thirsk, 10th August 2009

This is a poem about the aging process, and the realisation that it is happening to me. I was 47 years old when I wrote it. It was one of two poems I wrote on the same day, you will find the other at the end!

Preface

This book is the consequence of a conscious decision to change our way of life which we felt had become unsatisfactory. Many of us complain about our lot in life and often we cannot see a way to alter or improve our circumstances. We feel trapped and wish we could do more with our lives. If you are one of those people, perhaps this true account of escape from an ordinary suburban 9 to 5 routine to one of adventure on the high seas is for you.

By reading about our travels I hope that you will be, above all, entertained by our attempts to take on the world, and perhaps to see the everyday and the ordinary in different and new ways. I also hope that you may see how our approach to living and our philosophy have helped us to deal with life's challenges and that those ideas may be of some interest or use.

Finally this book is for those people who are curious about what we have done and how we have gone about it; it is for those who would like to do something similar, and especially for those who are living a life they want to change. This is the story of why we made a change, how we made it possible and how we are enjoying the results.

The text is essentially an edited version of the daily diary that we have kept since beginning to live on our sailing boat Drumlin. The structure of the book was, therefore, determined by where we have been and what we were doing, but the narrative does divide into reasonably distinct sections giving a basis for the demarcation of the chapters. Where the diary is being quoted, it is printed in *italics*. In addition to the actual diary, the text is interspersed with other information, observations, comments and quotations.

I have found the composition of poetry a rewarding and economical way of expressing in words my views and feelings over the years and some of these ditties and doggerel punctuate the text to create a little variety, colour and amusement, for as Thoreau said:

"There is no doubt that the loftiest written
wisdom is either rhymed, or in some
way musically measured..." ! [1]
Henry David Thoreau

My reason for self-publishing this work is that if it is worthy of being read then it should be available! I have, on principle, made no attempt to approach a publisher who would judge this, not by the content, but by its marketability; and profit is not my motive for publishing as I have no interest in making more money for myself than I require! All I ask is that I am acknowledged as the author and owner of this "intellectual property", and if anyone honours me by reading it, I will consider the time taken writing well spent, and I thank them for that.

I would like to express my thanks to my wife Claire, for her help, support and encouragement in writing this book and for her help in keeping the journal upon which this is based.

Andrew Dalby, Troon, 2014.

Notes

For the sake of consistency diary dates follow this convention:

1. Day, date , month and year;
2. Location,
3. Time if relevant,
4. Wind expressed as cardinal compass points from which the wind was blowing followed by numbers indicating Beaufort strength,
5. Weather,
6. Barometric pressure, and
7. The day number.

Quotations are centred, tapered and numbered in superscript.

References are presented in the Vancouver system with the page number of the book from which the quotation is taken at the end.

I include my own poetry not necessarily in chronological order, but where it compliment the text. There is sometimes a little background information to go with the poem which I include for the sake of interest. To separate these digressions I use –oOo- after which I return to the main text.

CHAPTER ONE

Prelude to Departure

"It is not easy to write in a journal what interests
us at any time, because to write it is
not what interests us." [2]
Henry David Thoreau

What makes a perfectly ordinary suburban couple sell their
house, quit their jobs, buy a boat and sail off into the sunset?
Ask a hundred people who have done it and you will get a
hundred different answers, but I suspect they will all have one
thing in common: a desire to be free. But free from what?
That is another question. Our definition of freedom is perhaps
dependent upon what it is that binds us. Put simply, freedom
is to be liberated from something that oppresses us. This is the
key point here. Claire and I had reached that point in our lives
when we knew we needed to do something different.

"The time has come for man to
set himself a goal." [3]
Nietzsche

Upon hearing what we have done a common remark
people often make to us is to say how brave they think we are
for all the things we have given up or left behind, as if we
have taken a great risk. Yes, perhaps we are engaging in an
activity involving risk. Anyone who goes on the water takes a
calculated risk, as does anyone who climbs into a car. It is not
the degree of risk that is necessarily the issue here, but the
degree of familiarity. Human beings often fear less that which
is common place, although it may be equally or even more

perilous than a danger we know less well. For me a normal life with its monotonous predictability and inevitability became the thing I feared most. The domesticated banalities of an homogenous modern day consumerist lifestyle, along with the associated popular values that seem important to the people who embrace it, are to me the stuff of nightmares. The daily treadmill that requires ever increasing dependence upon "the system" to survive is to me the oppressive tyrant of the human spirit; of *my* human spirit. A facile illustration of this is exemplified in the relationship I had with my car. I had to go to work in order to afford to run a car primarily so that I could go to work. Admittedly it is good to have a car for those occasional "social and domestic" journeys, but after taxing, insuring, maintaining and putting fuel into it, meant that the remaining financial reward from my work was almost cancelled out. Notice that it was *almost* cancelled out, but not quite enough to justify or enable me to stop work. So much of life is taken up with keeping up that it can get in the way of actually living and being.

" ... the cost of a thing is the amount of what I call life
which is required to be exchanged for it,
immediately or in the long run." [4]
Henry David Thoreau

Were we brave? No, we are not brave for deciding to change our way of life. The brave thing would have been not to, for as Nietzsche's Zarathustra said,

"I found life more dangerous among
men than among animals." [5]
Nietzsche

Up to the point of our departure in June 2012 our way of life had been quite unremarkable and ordinary in most respects. After graduating from Music College I spent the first twelve years of my career as a school teacher. I married Claire, my college sweetheart, after my first year as a secondary school teacher and we had three children; Martin our son in 1987, followed by our second son Neil in 1991, and Hannah our daughter in 1994. In 1995 I became a self-employed musician and private music tutor, and occasionally drove heavy goods vehicles to supplement my income, as a consequence of the one extraordinary event that occurred in our lives. Neil was diagnosed with acute lymphoblastic leukaemia. If there is one thing that has the ability to immediately and totally focus the mind of a parent on what is and is not important in life it is the threat of harm to one's child! Job, career, house, mortgage, car et cetera suddenly retreat to the boundaries and assume the insignificance that they deserve. All that matters is the child and the family, everything else becomes almost irrelevant. If I am honest at the age of 33 I had spent nearly a third of my life working with people with whom I had little if anything in common, and in some cases a dislike for, in a profession that, in my opinion, is poorly funded and over interfered with by the political classes, a profession that "could do better" where the future prospects of our offspring are concerned!

The first step, therefore, in my personal road to freedom was my escape from the teaching profession and all the inherent stresses, contradictions and disappointments it relentlessly ground into my life. I loved teaching, but teachers as a species I generally dislike with their limited horizons and often poor appreciation of "the real world". The means by which this change came about I would of course have gladly reversed. To have spared my son the life he endured I, like any parent, would have paid any price. The consequences of Neil's illness and death have had far reaching and profound effects on many people, and this story is an account of some

4

of the effect and influence he had on me. He taught me that life is unpredictable, we do not know how much of it we will be granted, and we must seize the day.

Do Something!

Whatever you do, pursue perfection and strive for excellence,
But do not let the fear of failure stop you from doing
anything!
Do something!
Move towards your goal,
For it is through action that we progress,
And to progress means that we are living out our lives.
But to do nothing is no life at all!

Andrew Dalby, Thirsk, 8th March 2006

Looking back through my life and observing how I approach problems and challenges I have noticed a peculiar characteristic. I like many people use lists to organise my life but I carry it to another level. I like to formalise them and I use mnemonics to assist in remembering them and to further systematise how I use them. This is all an attempt to find systematic and simplified ways of dealing with life. I think I began to use this approach as a teenager when I was learning to drive. My father was a police officer and trained to the advanced level required by Road Traffic Officers. They drive according to a system which he taught to me. In my late twenties I took up flying and as anyone who has been in an aircraft will know, pilots use sets of checks to be completed prior to, during, and after flight. These systems ensure that nothing is left to chance or overlooked, and assist in clear thinking in an emergency or tricky situation. They also make the activities logical; reduce them to the simplest and most efficient level of effort, and easier to remember. To me this is beauty, beauty in its purest form, which is elegant simplicity.

As my adult life progressed I found that it became progressively complicated, I had to juggle increasing numbers of balls and keep them all in the air at once, and the fear of dropping one introduces levels of anxiety that far outweigh the importance of the thing itself. The pressure of responsibility increases as we take on more of it. We have mortgages and loans, duties to perform at work, commitments to family, friends and often community organisations too, all ceaselessly clamouring for our time and energy, two commodities we all have in finite yet unknown and unquantifiable amounts. I craved simplification. I wanted a rest!

Things

Things,
Pretty things,
Useful things.
Things to make life easier,
Things to make me richer.
The richer I am the more things I have,
The more I have, things weigh me down,
Things bring me down,
Things slow me down,
Fewer things, easier road,
Travel with less,
No more things,
Lighter load.
Nothing!

Andrew Dalby, Thirsk, 10th August 2009

If one theme runs through my life it is this, a desire to be rid of clutter, to live a simple and simplified life. Consumerism and the daily grind of work required to feed the monster which is materialism is my daily foe.

> "... whoever possesses little is possessed
> that much less: praised be
> a little poverty!" [6]
> Nietzsche

-oOo-

I came to the conclusion in my thirties that I did not seem to really want what was expected of me. I had no desire to keep trading in my car for a newer and better model, or to sell my house for a larger one in a more desirable area. I didn't even want fancy foreign holidays, at least not the package style fortnight once a year in the sun. I wanted time and space, the freedom to do the things that mattered to me, time to be creative or to learn and explore or to meet people. I realised that material things were not what I wanted, I did not want "...treasures upon earth, where moth and rust doth corrupt" [7] which have to be paid for out of the wages paid by those who would deprive me of my time, my life. But I was trapped and could not see a way out.

> "But I foresee that if my wants should be
> much increased, the labour
> required to supply them
> would become a
> drudgery." [8]
> Henry David Thoreau

I vividly remember the morning Neil was diagnosed with leukaemia; it was Tuesday 21st March 1995. He had been bruising rather easily on his legs and a rash was appearing on his body. The former we put down to the daily rough and tumble of playing football with older boys and the latter we suspected was a socially contracted condition such as scabies, a not uncommon ailment in the school I was teaching in at the time which was in a deprived area of Scarborough. Claire soon returned with him from the doctor's surgery with instructions to attend the Children's Ward in the Friarage Hospital in Northallerton for a blood test. At this point we realised that something was seriously wrong. Very shortly afterwards the paediatrician, who had spent a number of years working in the paediatric oncology ward at St James's Hospital in Leeds, was able to tell us the result of the test. Neil had an abnormally high white blood cell count and severely depleted platelets. Platelets are the part of blood that heals wounds. Their absence was the reason for the ease with which he was bruising and was indicated by the rash, tiny blood blisters on the skin called petechia. She told us that other diseases can mimic leukaemia, but that this was highly unlikely and to be prepared for confirmation in Leeds that Neil had leukaemia. By mid afternoon my parents had come to Thirsk and taken charge of the house and Martin and Hannah; our good friend and native of Leeds, Eric, escorted us to the hospital and we found ourselves on the children's cancer ward. I never entered a classroom again as a teacher!

The following days, months and years were filled with heartache, joy, love and adventure. The heartache obviously caused by Neil's suffering and the tensions that created within the family; joy was the product of being made to live more in the moment and to enjoy being a family united in the common cause of making the most of our time together; love, we appreciate the love we feel for each other so much more when we have to face the possibility of the loss of a loved one; and adventure because every good day free from hospital, when Neil was well enough, presented an opportunity to live life to the full, so we did! In simple terms Neil's illness brought us closer together and focused our minds on what mattered, and we began to live life as well as we could in the circumstances.

"But man postpones or remembers; he does not live in the present, but with reverted eye laments the past, or, heedless of the riches that surround him, stands on tiptoe to foresee the future. He cannot be happy and strong until he too lives with nature in the present, above time." [9]
Ralph Waldo Emerson

One of our favourite pastimes was to take our canoe to Lake Windermere.

"Believe me, my young friend, there is *nothing*—absolute nothing—half so much worth doing as simply messing about in boats." [10]
The Wind in the Willows
Kenneth Grahame

When Neil was in the bone marrow transplant unit at St James's Hospital in April 1998 we read a book together on how to build a canoe out of plywood and we resolved to make this our summer project the following year once his treatment was over. The following February (1999), during a routine monthly visit to hospital for a check up, we learned that the transplant had not succeeded in eradicating the leukaemia and that no further options were left other than maintenance treatment and palliative care until such time as nature took its course. I took the consultant to one side and asked for his best guess as to how long Neil had to live. Naturally he could not say with any certainty so I made it easier for him by asking if 4 weeks was reasonable. He thoughtfully agreed it was. I then asked if 8 weeks was reasonable. He looked down and shook his head. This is terrible knowledge to possess, the knowledge of how long another person has to live, and as Neil was a child this was knowledge he should not have to own. I knew what I had to do; we were going to fit as much in to the coming days as was humanly possible.

The summer project was brought forward, and with a lot of help from Charles (Neil's Godfather), Richard (his Granddad) and many others too, we made the canoe in 6 days and she was launched on Windermere on the 7th day.

The 4 weeks passed then another 4, and another. It seemed almost to have been a mistake, but the routine blood tests still indicated that all was not well, but Neil continued quite well for another 20 months. During this time we had a small windfall from an insurance policy that matured and we had enough to buy a small inexpensive sailing boat.

It was early September 2000 and we had found "Rachel" a Seawych 19 for sale in Poole in Dorset. I was committed to play in a concert in Dulwich with "The Yorkshire Imps Band" on Saturday 9th September so we arranged with the broker that we would travel down to view the boat on Sunday 10th. The band's coach arrived back in Rothwell at about 10 pm and the arrangement was that Claire would pick me up in the car and bring me home. During the evening Neil started to feel unwell and he was running a temperature. This was not unusual, but his chemotherapy drugs had a suppressing effect on his immune system and a blood test was required under these circumstances to ascertain if he could fight off an infection himself or if he needed to be hospitalised for a course of intravenous antibiotics. These events had been a routine part of our life with leukaemia for over 5 years and, in the grand scheme of things, little more than a minor inconvenience. As it turned out Claire collected me from the coach and we all attended the Children's Ward in Leeds until the test results came back in the small hours. He had strong blood and did not need antibiotics this time. We arrived home at about half past 3 in the morning.

The children were all up quite early for a Sunday morning and despite having only had about 5 hours sleep I wandered downstairs at 9 am to be greeted by a very highly strung 9 year old boy pacing the dining room floor like an expectant father. "What time do you call this? We were supposed to be going to see a boat at 7 o'clock!" Neil was livid because we were not following the plan and the clock was ticking. I tried to reason with him and pointed out that last night he had been unwell. "That was last night!" I went on to explain that Thirsk to Poole is over 300 miles each way and we had to do it there and back before bedtime. His response was typical of Neil, and the look in his eye as good as said, "So what? Let's do it." By this time Claire had joined us and there was really no question as to how the day was going to proceed. I told the children to get into the car, Claire grabbed some food, I picked up my wallet and we set off. We arrived at the Ancasta Yacht broker in Poole at about 4 pm, their normal Sunday closing time, but they graciously remained behind to show us over the boat and explain the process of purchasing. By the time we had finished we had agreed that we would buy Rachel subject to a satisfactory survey. It was 7 pm. The salesman, who was used to brokering deals on yachts in excess of £250,000, had worked an extra 3 hours to sell us a £3500 boat!

A routine part of the monitoring process for Neil's condition was to examine the fluids in his spinal cord for signs of the disease hiding beyond the bloodstream and out of reach of the chemotherapy drugs, and to treat it there if necessary. Neil's next lumbar puncture, the final one of dozens he had endured, resulted in a small bleed into his spine because of his depleted platelets. The resulting pressure on the nerves caused paralysis from the waist down. He spent the remaining weeks of his life in a wheel chair and he died in hospital on Monday 23rd October 2000 of septicaemia. He never sailed in Rachel.

It is thanks to Neil's zest for life, his indomitable spirit and his formidable courage and determination that we ever came to own a proper sailing boat. We went on to enjoy a decade of sailing in the Clyde area based in Troon and to gradually build up experience and knowledge of the sea, all of which helped to prepare us for the adventure about to unfold. Unlike many popular tales of folks throwing caution to the wind our story would not make good reality television. We may be relatively inexperienced, but we are not inept or prone to theatrical tantrums. What follows is an account of a journey, the path of which was shown to us by a 9 year old boy who taught us that life is for living in the moment, it is not a rehearsal. After Neil died life returned to normal, as normal as it could be, but as the years rolled by our children grew up and left home and we found that we had less and less patience with the inconsequential minutiae of life and did not suffer its foolishness gladly. We had tasted life, we had learnt what matters and we were drowning in a sea of triviality. The time had come to put into practice the lessons we had learnt.

"... let us first be as simple as Nature ourselves, dispel
the clouds which hang over our own brows,
and take up a little life into our pores." [11]
Henry David Thoreau

Chapter Two

A New Beginning

"Hic trahunt naves ad mare. –
Here they drag the ships to the sea."
The Bayeux Tapestry circa 1070 -1077
Scene 36

Christmas 2010 was the first Claire and I had spent together without our children who by this time had both left home. We often talked about what we would do when the time came to retire which we had always assumed would not be for a few more years yet. As we thought about our circumstances over our Yuletide libations we began to realise that all our stars were aligned, and that if we were going to sell the house and buy a bigger boat to live on everything that needed to coincide had. We concluded that if we did not act now, we never would.

Over the following few weeks we sought up to date information about selling our house and using the proceeds to buy some properties to let. This way we would be able to keep a foothold on the property ladder, generate a small income and free up our assets to pay for a boat. All of the financial experts we consulted did not consider our plans unrealistic, so we went ahead. We calculated that our house, which we had just finished paying for after 25 years, would provide enough capital to buy a Westerly Konsort sailing boat outright, and leave enough to invest in 2 (perhaps 3 if we were careful) properties to let. We had reckoned that a boat of 29 feet in length was the optimum size for our needs; large enough to live on (just) and small enough that the running costs would be within the amount which we felt we could reasonably generate from our property investments. Our choice of the Konsort was no accident either. Not all boats are equal and we have found out by years of research, comparing many different boats in this size and price range that for our needs in terms of interior space, layout, sailing characteristics and performance there was no boat more suited to us than a Konsort. All we had to do was find the right one.

We also realised that we were going to have to be ruthless in reducing the quantity of possessions we had and to accept that we were going to have to live much more simply and cheaply than ever before. Giving away or throwing out much of our clutter was a liberating experience. I even found amongst my stuff a 1981 bank statement from my student days! We were going to have fewer demands on our money, but we were going to have much less of it. Our aim after meeting all our other obligations was to try to live on £30 a week for food.

> "Simplicity, simplicity, simplicity! I say, let your affairs be as two or three, and not a hundred or a thousand; instead of a million count half a dozen, and keep your accounts on your thumb nail." [12]
> Henry David Thoreau

On Tuesday 12th June 2012 we sold our house. There could be no turning back now!

Twenty Four Years Ago

Twenty four years ago...
If I could go back there again!
The thrill of youth and life spread forth,
And optimism untamed.

Twenty four years ago...
What did I know then?
I never thought the road I'd take
Would lead me here my friend!

Twenty four years ago...
Life seemed bright and so benign,
But now I'm here and worldly wise,
Its charm looks fake. Malign!

Twenty four years ago...
If I could go back there again
Would I do it differently?
Well that would all depend!

Twenty four years ago...
What other path to choose?
I know the way the first path led.
What have I to lose?

Twenty four years ago...
I chose the life I own.
I did the best I could back then.
I really shouldn't moan.

Twenty four years ago...
Had a different choice I made
Then who knows what my life would be?

No! I wouldn't trade.

Twenty four years ago…
Has made me what I am.
I wouldn't change the life I've had
And risk what I'll become.

Andrew Dalby, Thirsk, 26th May 2009

-oOo-

Tuesday 10th July 2012, Glasson Sailing Club, Lancaster:
Today we took possession of sailing yacht "Drumlin", a Westerly Konsort. Present at the handover were also Jean and Richard, Claire's parents, Pauline and Malcolm, my parents, and Martin and Lisa, our son and daughter in law.

Today also happened to be Jean's seventy third birthday, so we all adjourned to The Stork Hotel just outside the village for a celebratory meal. With the exception of our daughter Hannah, who was unable to be with us because of work, all the family were together for what was sadly to be the last time!

Wednesday 11th July 2012 Glasson Sailing Club, Day 1:
Today we returned to Drumlin with the car loaded full of the remainder of our possessions to bring aboard. Drumlin is now our home and main residence as we have decided to become liveaboards! Chip (my terrier) and Bracken (Claire's beagle) have also joined us on our adventure. Tonight is to be our first night in our new home.

Our good friends and neighbours, Sandi and Merv, are fellow sailors and have for many years spent their summers cruising their yacht Benita around the Mediterranean. As luck would have it their house was vacant at the time of the sale of ours and they kindly allowed us to live there for the few weeks it took us to buy Drumlin.

Thursday 12th July 2012 Glasson Sailing Club, Day 2:
Today we began searching through and exploring Drumlin's nooks and crannies. There is so much stuff here that we could open a chandlery! Claire sorted much of the interior and I fixed the anti-foul patches which had been scraped bare by the surveyor and we both replaced the anode which was rather "sacrificed"!

Boats have metal parts such as propellers and pipes that come through the hull and into the sea. Not all of these metal pieces are made of the same material and as you may recall from your school science lessons galvanic corrosion can happen. To prevent the important parts of the boat dissolving an electrical circuit is created; at one end of the wire is the precious part of the boat to be saved, usually the propeller and engine, and at the other a lump of metal called an anode usually made of zinc. The anode is mounted in line of sight of the propeller and beneath the waterline of course. When the boat is in the water the circuit is completed by the salt water and any current that flows carries away the zinc dissolving the anode instead of the boat!

I have never had to change an anode before and on the face of it the job is not difficult. Two studs are bolted through the hull and the anode is bolted onto the studs, simple. Six nuts are involved, if you don't count the one wielding the spanner, and a small wire connects the anode studs to the engine block. However, the diagram I had found on the internet did not correspond to the way the old anode had been fitted. To assist me in the fitting of the studs Claire had crawled into the dark recess of the cockpit locker and slithered under the cockpit sole into the confined space where the propeller shaft exits through the stern gland. Inverted and bent double she gripped the spanner securing the inside nuts whilst I tightened up the ones on the exterior. Doubt crept into my mind, and nearby were a group of fellow sailors enjoying a drink in the sunshine on the sailing club terrace, I felt it would be prudent to get a second opinion on my method, so I went over to obtain one. Six men, six broadly dissimilar opinions, and finally an admission from each sage in turn that not one of them had ever in fact fitted one either! I returned to Drumlin. I had forgotten to tell Claire where I was going and judging by the tone of the voice that responded to my lame apology for nearly half an hour's absence without leave, I was not likely to be forgiven in a hurry.

Monday 16th July 2012, Glasson Sailing Club, Day 6:
We have spent a quiet day reading instruction manuals and sorting things out. Claire made some coat hanger pockets to hang clothes in the wardrobe. The dogs seem very settled. We also did a big provisioning shop. We spent £40, £10 above our £30 budget, but we included things that we won't normally need to buy each week. We shall see how we get on financially. If we stick to the rule, which is to try to live on £30 per week we should manage to survive without frittering away our savings. Things should improve when the rental properties come on stream.

Tuesday 17th July 2013, Glasson Sailing Club, Day 7:
Our good friend and engineer Doug came over from North Wales today and we spent the day with tracing the plumbing to the seacocks and generally looking at the technical bits of Drumlin. We located all the through-hull fittings and, as far

as we are able to tell on the hard standing, they are all in working order. Doug left for home at 2pm and the rain arrived.

We have had our lifejackets for a number of years and we decided to test them, not by manually blowing them up as in the past but by firing them. They were in good order, but of course we needed new re-arming kits. I made the 10 minute walk into Glasson to visit the chandlery. Upon my return I discovered that I had bought the wrong type so I will have to return them tomorrow. Industry standardisation would go a long way to improving safety in such matters!

We listened for the 16.30 Liverpool Coast Guard weather forecast broadcast. They hailed on channel 16 and sent us to channel 23, which is normal radio procedure, and we spent 15 minutes listening to total silence, which is not! I am unsure what happened there and thank goodness for the internet as another source of information.

Tomorrow is to be launch day and high tide at our standard port Liverpool is 11.35. Glasson's high tide comes at Liverpool +25 minutes, so noon is the time to be going afloat. In anticipation I have located all the fenders and three warps. Tomorrow morning I shall clear the cockpit locker to ensure access to the stern gland which needs to be bled to ensure it is watertight.

Wednesday 18th July 2012, Glasson Basin Marina, Day 8:
Today at 11a.m. Drumlin was launched. Her previous owners assisted and accompanied us round to the marina and they helped us to get the feel of the boat. Everything went without incident and we were safely into the Glasson Basin marina by 12 noon.

Thursday 19th July 2012, Glasson Basin Marina, Day 9:
Today began by bending on the genoa then our friends Barbara and Trevor arrived for a visit, we had lunch with them and they stayed until late afternoon. We finished the day by finding and fitting the kicking strap mechanism onto the bottom of the boom. Claire cleaned off some more green from the woodwork on deck and looked out the dodgers and washed them.

Friday 20th July 2012, Glasson Basin Marina, Day 10:
Today our first job was to bend on the mainsail, Claire then cleaned off more green growth on the rubbing strake and toe rails and I worked out how the batteries are wired and cleared the quarter berth. Battery 1 is to start the engine, battery 2 is for the 12V domestic system.

Saturday 21st July 2012, Glasson Basin Marina, Day 11:
We cleaned out and flushed the water system, and discovered that the toilet holding tank "filler" cap is seized. It is really the emptying cap for use at pump out facilities in marinas. We fitted the life raft and the dodgers, and I tested the dinghy and outboard. I also took both dogs for a small ride in the dinghy under oars to see if they would like it or panic in a strange environment. They seemed to like it.

We were busy pondering something on deck when it occurred to Claire that it had gone rather quiet. She asked me if I had seen Bracken recently. No sooner had she asked than I looked along the pontoon to see him leaning over the edge and sniffing something on the water. As he did so his back legs came in transit with his front paws on the very edge. Before a word could be uttered he had pushed forward his nose a fraction too far upsetting his equilibrium. He fell in! It was only a matter of time. The score for dunkings stands at Bracken 1: Chip 0!

Claire has finished de-greening the toe rails and rubbing strake and has cleaned the cockpit. All in all a busy day and Drumlin is almost ready to go to sea!

Sunday 22nd July 2012, Glasson Basin Marina, Day 12:
Today we did more "housekeeping" cleaning and fitting the Man Overboard system and temporarily fitting the jack stays (safety lines), which have no obvious anchorage point forward. I also measured the lazy jacks (sail catcher when the main is lowered) in order to buy more 4mm rope to re-rig them because the old line was rotten. I did a full safety and security inspection as part of the "SHIPRIPS" protocol. Once we get into a proper routine with all the systems up and running a weekly "SHIPRIPS" should become a routine and organised matter. At the moment it's all a bit haphazard. NB "SHIPRIPS" is one of my mnemonics; security/safety, hull, interior, provisioning. "SHIP" is what to do. "RIPS" is how to do it; review (the log), inspect, prioritise and sign off when completed. Drumlin has a maintenance log kept separately.

Monday 23rd July 2012, Glasson Basin Marina, Day 13:
Today I went up the mast to thread the new lazyjack lines through the pulleys above the spreaders. About twenty feet up, barely half way and in a small marina! Not to be attempted at sea.

Claire baked buns very successfully in the oven, so another first there as well. I checked the fuel filter for signs of water in the fuel system, if it was correctly done the result was no water. I think it was. The engine anode has finally been tracked down, but as yet not examined or replaced. (Another smaller anode inside the engine itself.) *We are getting to know Drumlin better by the day. Soon we shall have an opportunity to sail her!*

Tuesday 24th July 2012, Glasson Basin Marina, Day 14:
Today Claire's sister, Bridget, and two Aunts, June and Vivienne came for lunch. We later left Drumlin for one last trip to finish things in Thirsk.

Thursday 26ᵗʰ July 2012, Glasson Basin Marina, Day 16:
We are back aboard Drumlin having been to Thirsk to remove the last of our belongings from Sandi and Merv's, house. We have a few belongings that we do not wish to dispose of but cannot keep on the boat, so tomorrow I shall drive the car and its contents up to my cousin Robert's house near Kilmarnock and leave it there until we arrive in Troon by boat, we can then take it the rest of the way to Inverness to store it with Claire's parents. I will return to Glasson by Train on Saturday and then we should just about be ready to set sail.

The Friday 27ᵗʰ July 2012 was the day of the opening ceremony for the Olympic Games in London. Quite a spectacle!

Sunday 29ᵗʰ July 2012, Glasson Basin Marina, Lancaster, Day 19:
We spent the day pottering. I began to outline plans for the passage to Ramsey on the Isle of Man and spent a couple of hours trying to work out why the central heating won't work! At least we discovered how to set the time on it and what the big pull out knob under the switch and fuse panel does. It lights the heater buttons up for night time use. I also dismounted, reset, replaced and reprogrammed the Navtex. Now it is working!

Navtex is a device that receives digital weather and navigational information in text format. You can read it when it is convenient and does not depend upon stopping what you are doing to listen to the radio.

I also dipped a lead line over the stern to discover that we are in 2.3 metres of water. The depth gauge is reading 1.3 meters, so its offset is to the bottom of the keels. Add one meter for the actual depth of the water.

The offset is useful because it is better to know how much water there is under the boat so you don't bump into things or the bottom. Rather than just knowing the depth. For example if the depth is 1 meter Drumlin would be aground. If we know there is 1 meter beneath the keels we would still be floating, and the water would actually be about 2 meters deep!

We also ran out of water today, so a tank full has been used in a week. It is useful to know how long we can be away from a water source.

Monday 30th July 2012, Glasson Basin Marina, Day 20:
I went to Lancaster and back by bus to do the week's shopping, Claire stayed aboard and finished stowing and tidying up in readiness for Norman and Elizabeth's visit.

Norman and Elizabeth arrived mid afternoon and we had an evening of food, chat and company. They are staying the night, our first overnight guests!

Tuesday 31st July 2012, Glasson Basin Marina, Day 21:
We spent a lovely day with Norman and Elizabeth who seemed to enjoy their stay aboard Drumlin as our first guests. They left for home in the evening.

Wednesday 1st August 2012, Glasson Basin Marina, Day 22:
Most of today has been spent considering whether or not to set off for the Isle of Man tomorrow. All the plans have been made and our final decision depends upon the weather forecast tomorrow.

Thursday 2nd August 2012, Glasson Basin Marina, Day 23:

I slept badly. Last night walking the dogs before bed I actually felt "Spooked" walking the pontoons between familiar boats! During the night I had a nightmare about when Neil died all mixed up with him being alive and older. Not nice! On balance I think I was anxious about whether to sail to the Isle of Man, how the passage would be weather wise and if my skills and experience were up to taking a newer, bigger and unfamiliar yacht to sea for the first time in some of Britain's most dangerous and challenging waters.

First thing this morning Claire and I discussed our options, reviewed the forecast and decided to go!

Casting off proved easy enough, and as we were considering how to moor up to wait for the lock keepers they opened the gates and beckoned us in. But, Drumlin's engine note suddenly changed and "smoke" started wafting from her stern. Now, the previous owner did say that she "steamed". We decided to press on. We later discovered that the "knocking" engine note was in fact not from the engine, but was a cockpit locker hasp vibrating sympathetically and the smoke was normal steam caused by the cooling water being heated by the exhaust gases.

The engine is cooled by drawing sea water into the engine and after it has rinsed through the cooling system it is sent back to the sea via the exhaust pipe.

The day turned out a great success. The sea was slight and the wind negligible. The tide carried us swiftly and not too dramatically out of the river Lune to sea and towards the Isle of Man. As evening approached our speed slowed as the tide turned but we never dropped below 3.5 knots. Claire took the helm as we turned west out of the Lune and stayed there until about 18.00hrs. I did the navigation, log keeping and galley duties. The dogs behaved magnificently.

20.00 hrs saw the official start of night sailing just as the Isle of Man began to loom large. By the time we were around Moughold Head into Ramsey bay night had taken hold, the sea rose to moderate and the wind was blowing fresh. We entered Ramsey harbour at midnight. Every available space was taken by fishing vessels so we went out to the visitors' moorings by the derelict Queens Pier. Claire superbly picked up the mooring second time round, the first attempt being aborted when our new boat hook came to pieces bashing her face in the process. No real harm done. Sixty some miles safely covered in thirteen hours. As there had been no wind we motored all the way. So far we have not sailed Drumlin!

Friday 3rd August 2012, Ramsey Harbour, Isle of Man, Day 24:

What a night! The visitor moorings here are a rough place in an easterly force 5. We have also found out that Drumlin has a couple of vices that we need to cure her of. Firstly the anchor clatters when a mooring line is lead through the other side of the bow roller, and secondly the metal water tank beneath the forepeak bed bangs like a bass drum when the water inside sloshes. Some deadening patches may reduce it, but when the rigging wires drone and wail in the wind and the tank pounds its inconsistent rhythms it is like trying to sleep through a Scottish pipe and drum band rehearsal for beginners and novices with no musical ability whatsoever!

Claire awoke with a bad headache which rapidly deteriorated to something between a migraine and seasickness. We decided to try the harbour again and were greeted by chirpy and helpful staff who opened the swing bridge to let us in. Here we executed yet another first in our sailing career; we rafted up alongside another yacht called "Tidewinder" against a wall in a harbour that dries and at the height of a 9.4 meter tide. Four hours later, and some 30 feet lower, Drumlin and her neighbour gently and without fuss settled firmly on the sea bed. Having spent the time fiddling and adjusting mooring warps and fenders she is now able to be safely allowed to rise and fall with the others while we sleep tonight. And sleep we shall as we are very tired.

The dogs behaved impeccably.

Saturday 4th August 2012, Ramsey, Day 25:
We awoke with a start this morning as Drumlin gave a shuddering bang. We rushed on deck expecting to have caught Tidewinder's rubbing strake or to find a mooring warp snapped or something. Nothing! Inside we tore open the saloon lockers to access the keel bolts to see if the weight of the boat on her keels was damaging her hull. Nothing! There was nothing to suggest anything was wrong at all. Bang again – It could only be stones or pebbles dislodging beneath the starboard keel as Drumlin's weight gradually came to bear on the sea bed. And so back to bed!

A later closer inspection of the river bed, the river Sulby flows out to sea through the harbour at Ramsey, along the harbour wall where we were moored up revealed a lot of flat fragments of slate. The gunshot like reports we were hearing were the fracturing of small pieces of stone as Drumlin bedded down with each ebb of the tide.

We waited for the tide to rise and when we felt able to scale the harbour wall ladders whilst carrying dogs we went ashore. We reconnoitred Ramsey whilst walking the dogs and found the usual selection of supermarkets and convenience stores. A quick trip back home to make a shopping list and we returned to do a shop for fresh food.

Whilst Claire made lunch I filled the water tank and put our newly bought £3 prepaid electricity card into the meter. Result? No electricity! Reason, I'd put it in the wrong slot and topped up next door's account! This is the result of tiredness and a lack of concentration. We bought another and tried again. Success!

This evening we took the dogs for another walk on the north beach and let them off for a run. My old English teacher once said, "The definition of a lady is a woman who paints her toenails even if she is going to wear shoes." I mention this as Ramsey, like Rothesay, Scarborough and Bridlington for example, is very similar in architectural style and vintage. Often times these buildings look tired from the front and positively unhygienic from behind the facade. But my impression of Ramsey is that she is a "lady". Fresh paint, none of it peeling, and not just the obvious bits you can see. Mooragh Lake with her parkland and surrounding fence is immaculate. I found the atmosphere here to be strangely continental, somehow not English, yet the local accent is somewhere between Lancastrian and Liverpool. Well done Isle of Man for staying unique and preserving your sense of identity, and for resisting being absorbed into the homogeneity of Anglo-American conformity and uniformity.

This evening the lifeboat service was having a gala on the south promenade. We walked round. They were having motorcycle races on the sand, hence the noise we were hearing! Even children of primary school age on miniature motorcycles were bouncing over jumps and sliding round sandy corners at full tilt and occasionally falling off and jumping right back on. At the end of the races smiles as wide as the beach itself, and covered in almost as much sand, stretched across the faces of those who had been taking part. In fact there were races for riders of all ages and skill levels. There were also burger and hotdog stalls and fancy goods for sale all to raise money for charity. Excellent community fun! There is something a bit motorbike friendly around here. I can't think why!

Sunday 5th August 2012, Ramsey, Day 26:

Today I made plans for our passage to Portpatrick on the west coast of Scotland. By happy coincidence Tidewinder's owner arrived and we exchanged pleasantries about mooring alongside and about our new way of life. Her skipper was a very open and friendly gentleman who spent time giving us local insight into strategies for rounding the Point of Ayre at the north end of the Isle of Man and for tackling the Mull of Galloway. His advice was invaluable and we are grateful for the time and trouble he took to share his knowledge with us.

The dogs have had a couple of long walks today, they don't like being abseiled up and down the quay wall at low tide, but they do enjoy the results!

Monday 6th August 2012, Ramsey, Day 27:

It has been a warm and sunny day. Ramsey is growing on us as a place, in fact the limitation of climbing on and off Drumlin is the only downside. I recommend the Isle of Man as a "must see before you die" holiday destination! The Harbour Keeper, Mr Swales, is a gentleman of the highest order, nothing is too much trouble for him. He even came to us to take away our out of date flares and an unwanted jerry can.

Today we fuelled and oiled Drumlin ready for departure and bought in the last of the provisions. Tomorrow we shall confirm the weather forecast and if it is as expected we shall go out of the harbour and on to a swinging mooring at Queens Pier ready for a clear start on Wednesday. Who knows? We may even sail her in the bay tomorrow afternoon just for fun!

I just remembered, I saw my first Manx cat last night when walking the dogs. They didn't see it though because they didn't try to chase it!

Tuesday 7th August 2012, Ramsey Bay, Day 28:
Today we bade farewell to Ramsey harbour after a leisurely morning walking the dogs, topping up the water and a good lunch. I went to Mr Swales the Harbour Keeper's office to pay our dues and to negotiate when the swing bridge would let us out. We decided upon 4pm local time (I always use GMT on the boat, we call it ship's time.) and he said he would come and visit us to see if we were ready before opening the bridge. Nothing was too much trouble.

We left the harbour and ventured out on to a mirror like sea with no wind. More in hope than expectation we hoisted the sails which hung as limp and motionless as dead fish, and Drumlin remained serenely but emphatically stationary. Officially we are yet to sail her!

We returned to the same mooring that we tied to last Thursday and spent the evening enjoying the panoramic view of Ramsey, the faint outline of Scotland and a clear view of the Lake District. It isn't every day that you can see two different countries across the sea at the same time from what is almost another country in its own right. The Isle of Man sounds like Liverpool, feels like France and looks like Scotland: it is a truly "different" place.

Wednesday 8th August 2012, Portpatrick, Scotland, Day 29:
We arrived in Portpatrick at 21.00 hrs ship's time and at low tide. It has been a calm, even simple crossing without incident. The effects of the tide are alarming, we were cruising at about 4 knots but the GPS indicated that we were doing in excess of 7 knots over the ground at one point which means that the water was carrying us along at 3 knots.

In other words if we had stopped dead in the water we would still have been travelling at 3 knots. About walking speed!

You have to work with the tide, especially in a sailing boat!

I am very annoyed with myself – Drumlin touched the bottom unintentionally in the harbour when I was turning the boat around. What a black hole at night! At least we are safely in.

The sailing literature we had read suggested that the inner harbour at Portpatrick had been upgraded for the leisure boat visitors by the provision of pontoon berths. For whatever reason this turned out not to be the case and Portpatrick has no modern berthing facilities available to visitors. The entrance into the harbour is tricky, especially in the dark as the entrance is narrow and difficult to see at night. Accuracy on approach is required to avoid the rocks. Once inside the natural harbour, which has a small beach within it, a 90° turn to the left takes you into the old harbour, a deep, sheer sided rectangular hole with a few ladders built into the wall for crew to scale up with mooring lines. Because I had not expected to have to head for one of these ladders my approach was all wrong so I decided to execute a figure of eight manoeuvre anticlockwise in the inner harbour and clockwise outside to set up my new approach. Once in the outer harbour and turning towards the beach, mistakenly believing it would be safer to turn away from it into deeper water, I ran out of depth, in a hurry. Fortunately sand and a slow speed made for a soft majestic genuflection towards the promenade, and a cough of reverse power shuffled us backwards off the bottom, whereupon we completed the exercise with no further loss of dignity.

Finally we made it alongside and I held Drumlin securely to the ladder whilst Claire climbed up with the mooring lines. There are few secure points to tie on to, and those that are there are relics of the old days of sail when Portpatrick was the main ferry port for Northern Ireland. Upon her conquest of the summit, Claire was greeted by an Irish gentleman a little worse for wear who insisted that he knew Drumlin and that she was from Strangford Lough. No amount of persuasion could convince him we had come from Glasson! Interestingly we had been initially mistaken for another Irish vessel called Drumlin in Ramsey too. We have concluded that we are not alone! The gentleman eventually took his leave, much to the relief of my tired arms, allowing Claire to finally secure our lines.

Thursday 9th August 2012, Portpatrick, Day 30:
It is a long way up the harbour wall ladder at low tide, but we had to do it and hoist the two dogs up for a walk. Bracken was in mad mode. We walked around the harbour to the islet. He barked at any dog in sight, and there were plenty. Back at the lifeboat pier whilst barking at a black cocker spaniel puppy his lead broke. He darted towards it, nipped its ear and described a large circle without taking his eyes off his quarry. Unfortunately for Bracken the diameter of his circle exceeded the width of the pier. After a gravity assisted flight of twenty feet or so we heard a splash. How he managed to miss the moored boat and the lifeboat jetty we don't know. A lifeboat man on the boat below shouted up to say the dog was okay and promptly fell overboard trying to rescue him ruining his

new state of the art mobile phone in the process. I paid the harbour fees and we left a couple of hours later, praying that we would not require the services of Portpatrick lifeboat!

The score for dunkings now stands at Bracken 2: Chip 0!

Once again we motored all the way on this the third leg of our journey to Troon. We used the autohelm to steer us most of the way and the chart plotting GPS ran out of data just north of Ailsa Craig. It's a good job we have paper charts. Lady Isle light house 2 miles west of Troon was easy enough to identify, but Troon Harbour entrance is awkward to make out in the dark when approaching from the south east because of all the clutter of street lights. We arrived just after 1am local time.

We are here!

Friday 10th August 2012, Troon Yacht Haven, Scotland, Day 31:
It is our 27th wedding anniversary.

After a little lie in we had breakfast and tidied up. Later in the morning we had a visit from my cousin Robert and his family, Lynn and children Don and Debs, followed shortly afterwards by my Auntie Jenny and her friend Edna. In the afternoon we made arrangements with the marina to berth Drumlin here over winter. We then celebrated our wedding anniversary with fish and chips from "The Wee Hurrie", an award winning and highly regarded fish restaurant by Troon harbour, accompanied by a bottle of wine.

Today the weather has been scorching hot. Summer has shown her face at last. We also texted and e-mailed a few folks "back home" to let them know we have arrived safely. I checked the fuel again today. Drumlin seems to consume fuel at the rate of about 2 litres per hour and our average speed over 160 nm was 4.3 knots. I calculate that that is about a third of a tank in ten hours motoring.

Chapter Three

Summer in the Clyde

Requiem aeternam dona
eis, Domine, Et lux
perpetua eis.

Saturday 11th August 2012, Troon, Day 32:
My cousin Robert and his children Debs and Don came for a sail in Irvine Bay with me this morning and Claire went with Lynn back to their house to do the laundry. At 3 pm Claire returned with the washing mostly dried and we set sail due west for Lamlash. Originally we had planned to go North West to Millport, but southerly winds were forecast which make it an uncomfortable place to moor because it gets rough. The crossing was good and we managed to sail for the first couple of miles, but the wind dropped when we were west of Lady Isle so we had to put the engine on. For the first time since coming aboard Drumlin we reached our destination in daylight. We settled down to a good dinner and then to bed. During the early hours the wind strengthened and Drumlin began tugging on the mooring line so we lengthened it and reduced the snatching considerably. I wrenched my arm whilst trying to make the adjustments but the result was a much more comfortable motion to the boat.

Sunday 12th August 2012, Lamlash, Isle of Arran, Day 33:
It has been a lazy day. We woke up to a dull and overcast sky with a swell coming from the east mixed up with a blustery easterly wind. It is calmer now.

For the last few days I have been pondering what to routinely include in this log. Up until now I have recorded the date, the location and the day number. Perhaps I should include weather and barometer readings and other details so that when a year has passed it would be interesting to look back and compare. I could also mention other points of interest like history for example. If a place has significant history it will give me a focal point to guide me in reading and research! Kingscross point here on Arran for example has an early and fairly unusual Viking grave comparable only to those on Colonsay! King Haakon anchored his fleet here in Lamlash in 1263 when he was harassing Alexander III of Scotland. Negotiation failed and a small skirmish ensued at Largs. The Norwegians considered this a "withdrawal", the Scots a victory. As is normal in these things the victors write the history.

Free Night 1

A major objective in our new lifestyle is to gain greater independence, increase our self-sufficiency and reduce our living costs. Tying up in marinas is okay for the average yachtsman who perhaps sails for a few weeks a year as part of his annual holiday. Such a sailor would probably consider £25 per night a reasonable fee to pay, as would the average caravan and camping enthusiast. Multiply this sum up to 183 nights of a 6 month summer cruise and it would cost £4575, almost as much as renting a small house for a year! It is an economic imperative that we make best use of our anchor and park up for free.

Monday 13th August 2012, Port Bannatyne Marina, Isle of Bute, Baro 1011 Day 34:
It has been a showery grey day with force 3-4 SE winds and a moderate sea.

Today we moved from Lamlash to Bute. We motored for the first eight to ten miles but the breeze freshened and the genoa took over giving us 5.9 knots at one point. By Ascog Patch the wind had become erratic so we put the engine on, which promptly overheated! One new impellor later and lots of sea water into the coolant filter header tank and normal service was resumed.

Lesson learned:
Always look for cooling water exiting the exhaust pipe on initial start up.

As a result of the overheating incident I started thinking about how to avoid making the same mistake again and the result was a start up procedure. I considered all the factors necessary on Drumlin before actually turning the ignition key and came up with another one of my mnemonics. BELFIRST!

- Battery, select the correct one for starting.
- Engine, check the oil.
- Lines and lifejackets, prepare mooring warps for departure and don safety gear.
- Fuel, check you have sufficient.
- Instruments, turn them on.
- Radio, turn it on.
- Start up.
- Temperature, check the coolant is flowing through the engine.

We made a slightly undignified berthing at Port Bannatyne at about 5pm local time, but once neatly tied up we found ourselves next to a Norwegian flagged vessel. As a wheeze I hoisted my large Norwegian flag from the back stay and retreated under the spray hood to await a response. A few moments later the skipper Kjiel, a retired lighthouse keeper from Kristiansand, entered into conversation with me. Claire and I spent the remainder of the evening aboard "Eberth", a beautifully converted vessel, the interior of which is like a Norwegian cottage. The exterior is more utilitarian, but form and function match just fine. She started this life twenty years ago when Kjiel bought her, she was a prototype oil rig evacuation life boat. Basically she was a seventy seat fibreglass torpedo shaped escape pod come life boat. She is now a luxury, go anywhere bespoke yacht with a welcoming and easy going free spirit of a skipper who refuses to call what he described as his "Ugly boat" she, as that would be insulting to women! Well Claire and I like his boat and we do not think she is at all ugly. She is a tough, feisty and classy old girl, ample in size if plain in looks, but with a homely interior and a heart of gold. Well done Kjiel! It is to meet folks like you that we chose this way of life!

A Toast to Friendship

Here's to all the people that I have ever known,
And here's to all those people that I am yet to know.
To all those friends who've spared some time,
To all those friends who came to dine,
To all those friends who's smiles did shine,
And made my moments so.

Here's to all the people that shared their skills with me,
And here's to all those people that loved and cared for me.
To all those friends who give their all,
To all those friends who come to call,
To all those friends both large and small,
Who make my moments grow.

Here's to all the people I'll meet in times to come,
And here's to all those people across whose paths I'll run.
To all those friends who'll love me then,

To all those friends my faults will ken,
To all those friends who will be, when
At last my moments go.

To all those people ...

Andrew Dalby, Troon, 8th February 2013.

This poem came one day whilst reminiscing about people I had recently left behind when my thoughts wandered to people in my distant past. I began to realise how many had passed through my life, how many were still a part of it, and how that experience promised many more friends yet to be made. I felt optimistic!

-oOo-

Tuesday 14th August 2012, Port Bannatyne Marina, Day 35:
Today Neil would have celebrated his 21st birthday ... Probably with a BIG party! Perhaps we are here today because all those years ago he insisted that we go to see "Rachel" our previous boat, our first boat, in Poole in Dorset a few weeks before he died. We are certainly different from the people we would have been had we not done what he asked, and we are probably much better off and happier as a result. Thank you Neil!

We moved round to a swinging mooring in Rothesay Bay at lunch time. We launched the dinghy and I went ashore to do some shopping.

Wednesday 15th August 2012, Rothesay Bay Moorings, Baro 996, Day 36:

The weather is calm now and it has stopped raining. We have had force 5 and 6 winds with gusts of force 7 and rough water. The dinghy has taken a pounding off our stern, but lengthening her lines softened the effects somewhat. We have not been able to leave Drumlin today because the weather was too bad, but we did manage to spend time removing some more of the green slime from the cockpit between showers.

The Waverly came into Rothesay twice today. She is a sight to behold.

Built in 1946 the Waverley is the world's last sea going paddle steamer still carrying passengers, a replacement for the 1899 ship of the same name which sank during the Dunkirk evacuations in 1940.

I signed SY Drumlin up to FaceBook tonight as a way of quickly telling folks, family and friends, who are interested where we are. I am not sure if it will catch on with me, I am a little technophobic.

Thursday 16th August 2012, Rothesay Bay Moorings, Baro 1008, Day 37:

Today has been fine, sunny at times and much calmer. Claire and I went ashore in the dinghy with the two dogs, They, the dogs, managed well. Rothesay Council's Bute Berthing Company no longer look after the moorings, and now there are fewer of them than before and they are managed privately. Apparently the moorings didn't pay their way and of course the Bute Berthing Company has its swish new marina to promote in the inner harbour. It is all getting a bit too "exclusive".

Free Night 2

Friday 17th August 2012, At Anchor in Blackfarland Bay, Baro 1003, Day 38:

We woke up this morning to very poor visibility, heavy rain between showers and light winds. The plan for today was to leave Rothesay about 2 hours before high water in order to go through the Kyles of Bute with a favourable tide, so at 10.30 we made ready and set off northwards. We have been through the Kyles at least 3 times before on our own. It is a straight forward enough passage when timed correctly, but I still fail to enjoy the scenery as getting the course right through the narrows is so important!

Yesterday Claire and I had decided to aim for the anchorage at Blackfarland bay. The obvious place to anchor in this area is Caladh Harbour, but as it is as popular as a McDonalds drive though on a Saturday night we didn't think testing our ground tackle and our hither to rarely practised anchoring skills there would be a wise decision.

We arrived on station to anchor at 13.30hrs ship's time and anchored without drama. I am cautious by nature and felt it prudent to attach a tripping line to the anchor just in case it fouled something on the sea bed but I under measured the length of tripping line by a couple of meters. As we had arrived just after high tide, a wait of a couple of hours soon reunited us with our beloved pick up buoy which rose to the surface with the poise and dignity of the hand that offered Arthur Excalibur. We also laid out all 40 metres of our anchor chain, just in case! The last time Drumlin sat so still she was on the hard at Glasson sailing club.

We are opposite Tighnabruaich, the view is spectacular and so far the evening is still. Herons are fishing a few yards away on the shore. This, today, is our backyard, the reason we swapped bricks and mortar for GRP. And to top off the day our daughter Hannah rang to say that she has been promoted at work! Well done Hannah!

Free Night 3

Saturday 18th August 2012, Blackfarland Bay, Baro 1008, Day 39:

Today, according to BBC Radio 4 weather service, has been the hottest of the year so far. Certainly we have enjoyed settled and sunny conditions and as I write a red sky promises another fine day tomorrow. We survived our first night at anchor without incident, and shared the bay with a sloop and a ketch. We have also been neighbours to a large motor yacht with young people enjoying using the tender for waterskiing. Already this may conjure up images of loutish youths shattering the peace and tranquillity of the bay with noise and wake from their boat, but nothing could be further from the truth. They have been quiet and considerate, not to mention very entertaining to watch. It was clear from the courteous way they spoke to each other that the people concerned were not the sort to do anything but pilot their boat with due regard for those of us quietly at anchor. They judged when and how close to approach if they had to, and above all, when they had made enough noise, to stop before anyone could reasonably complain. My point is that there is room for all water sports to live together if the various interest groups are considerate and accommodating of each other. As in all things, it's the few that spoil it for the many.

At low tide I rowed the dinghy out to rescue the pickup buoy on the tripping line. Our old friend the Waverly called at Tighnabruaich today, complete with a piper to herald her arrival.

Free Night 4

Sunday 19th August 2012, Ardmarnock Bay Lower Loch Fyne, Baro 1014, Day 40:

It has been mostly overcast today with a force 3 or 4 southerly or south westerly wind.

We said our goodbyes to Blackfarland and motored into wind southwards until we were clear of Ardlamont Point where we turned west and hoisted full sail for the first time. Drumlin made 5 knots and pointed well to windward. She is a well mannered vessel and in a force 4 doesn't heel too much.

It has been a number of years since we last sailed in Loch Fyne. We decided to head for Ardmarnock Bay. We knew about the submerged rocks at the south of the entrance from the charts and pilot books so we gave them a wide berth as it was just after high water when we arrived. Once anchored, we watched as the tide ebbed away. We were glad that we had played safe as the rocks extend quite a way out. As I write this we are on the flood tide and our depth didn't go below 5 metres. All the chain is out so we need to keep a close eye on our swinging circle, the depth gauge alarms are set on guard and the air is quite still.

Free Night 5

Monday 20th August 2012, Ardmarnock Bay, Baro 1014, Day 41:

It is raining torrentially! The wind has been a southerly force 3 and until now it has been cloudy.

Now, did I mention the compass? Leaving Glasson it quickly became obvious that the compass was errant to put it politely. As we have a Global Positioning System, a chart plotter, paper charts and a hand held compass aboard it was not an issue as we knew not to rely on it. I had been researching the instruction book for the "Plastimo Contest" compass on how to correct it. However, the other day, Claire, being naturally inquisitive, grabbed a bit on the back of the compass, pulled it out, and Jack Horner like had extracted the plum which is the correction magnets. Examining it, my newly acquired theoretical knowledge immediately allowed me to deduce that the magnets had been "adjusted", presumably so that the compass would always point in the same direction. The wrong direction! I restored them to neutral and the compass now does a very good job of reliably pointing north and indicating with tolerable accuracy the direction the boat is heading. We know this as now the GPS and compass sing the same song at the same time. A much more harmonious ensemble.

18.15hrs, Baro 1014:
The rain turned to hail and lasted a good while then it brightened up, that is when we saw the Sun Odysee 42 "Skua" approaching to anchor. There were six aboard, half being teen-aged boys. The anchor was lowered as was the chain all in a heap! Minutes later the inflatable dinghy was cast off the sugar scoop stern and the boys were in fishing, most notably the one named Cameron, who for reasons best known to him refused to wear a life-jacket and announced to all who could hear, "Am no stoopit!". Now, is it just me or does anyone else think that sharp hooks and inflatable boats don't make the best of combinations? Very few minutes passed before the suicidal instinct of the local perciformes scombridae, mackerel to you and me, kicked in and they were queuing up to be hauled aboard and fried. This was quite entertaining to watch along with the family of six wet suited souls frolicking in the bay by the beach on a couple of body boards and yet another inflatable dinghy.

Free Night 6

Tuesday 21st August 2012, East Loch Tarbert Loch Fyne, Day 42:

As a strong south westerly with torrential rain was forecast we decided that Tarbert seemed a good idea to go and shelter. We also needed provisions so we came in. Shopping done, the weather quickly turned and confirmed that our decision had been a good one!

Magnus III Barefoot King of Norway (1073 -1103) managed to convince Malcolm III of Scotland that he could sail his ship around part of Scotland in a day. Malcolm agreed that if he did he could have the land so circumnavigated. Magnus sailed south from East Loch Tarbert, went west around the Mull of Kintyre, dashed north past the island of Gigha and swung starboard into West Loch Tarbert from whence he carried his ship over the land back into the village on the east side where he began his mission thus securing possession of the southern Kintyre Peninsular for the next 12 years! Tarbert is a common enough name in Scotland and means "Take boat" indicating a portage point over land between waterways creating useful shortcuts for journeys.

Two centuries later Robert the Bruce was to do a similar thing in the Scottish war of independence apparently!

Tarbert has been around for a long time, as early as 836AD it is mentioned in the Annals of Ulster (which cover AD 431 to AD 1540) as an important landing place for herring fishermen, and in the 18th century Thomas Pennant, a Welsh scholar, recorded ships of 10 tonnes being portaged over the isthmus! James Watt later surveyed the area declaring it feasible for an east to west canal, but delays meant that the Crinan project got there first. Quel dommage!

Wednesday 22nd August 2012, Tarbert, Baro 1011, Day 43:

There have been heavy showers and a breeze today. We spent our time relaxing, watching the world go by and enjoyed a walk around the town. We also turned our thoughts to our new property business and reviewed our progress towards that.

Thursday 23rd August 2012, Ardmarnock Bay, Day 44:
We have decided that we like it here; it is a pretty and quiet bay. I made a list of jobs to do in the maintenance log and set about an audit of our electrical ampere consumption from the specifications in the operator's manuals for each piece of equipment aboard. Claire continues to knit cushion covers and to test designs for her own knitting patterns.

Free night 7

Friday 24th August 2012, Bagh Buic (Buck Bay), Baro 999, Day 45:
We decided to vacate Ardmarnock in favour of the next but one bay, Bagh Buic, to the south of us due to the fact that the wind was veering through the north to the north east. This is a charming, even beautiful, bay with two big houses on the shore. The evening is really still and calm; in fact the weak tide has turned Drumlin on her anchor chain so that her stern is to the tripping line buoy above the anchor. This morning all the weather seemed to miss us, but it threw it down on the west side of the loch.

My little terrier Chip has been a clown today dressing up in his blanket. He has chewed a hole in the middle through which he put his head to wear it like a cloak. He looked like Yoda the Jedi Knight!

Other news – That man in Norway was sentenced to 21 years and declared sane and responsible for his actions. Well done

Norway, you have demonstrated to the world how to respond to terrorism. America and Britain TAKE NOTE!

Free Night 8

I will mention here that I could not bring myself to write the name of Norway's mass murderer in Drumlin's log book, but it is perhaps right to put this entry into context. I make no secret of the fact that I am a huge fan of Norway and Norwegians. It is a country that I love and have done since boyhood, I have visited many times, and it is a nation I admire in so many respects, although I do accept that they, like all others, have their faults. If Norway had reacted as stupidly to their big terror event on 22 July 2011 as America did to 9/11 and Britain to 7/7 the Norwegians could have concluded that, as Anders Behring Breivik claimed to have links with and was influenced in part by the English Defence League (a claim EDL strenuously deny), it would be reasonable for Norway to bomb Bradford or Luton and invade the UK. But then they do have their own oil. Many people could not understand the dignity and civility with which the Norwegians conducted the trial. That is perhaps because we in the UK are slowly and dangerously allowing public opinion to lose sight of what the law is there to do. The law in Britain, unless I am woefully mistaken, exists for justice NOT vengeance. That is why civilised countries do not have the death penalty. And if that point of view offends anybody, I really don't care. I'm with the Norwegians on this. Breivik was sentenced by the Oslo District Court to 21 years <u>preventive detention</u> with the option to keep him locked up as long as he is deemed to be a danger to society. In reality he will probably never be freed from prison for murdering 77 people.

Saturday 25th August 2012, Troon, Day 46:
It had been our intension today to relocate to Millport on the southern end of Great Cumbrae, but when we arrived we

found the bay full. With poor weather forecast from Monday onwards, we made for Troon. The weather is the main deterrent for staying out and the cause of us having to pay a week's berthing fees at full summer time rates in the marina. On the plus side we can take our new houses on from Friday 31st August and hopefully start making a little income from property rental.

Sunday 26th August 2012, Troon, Day 47:
Today we retrieved our car with the few possessions we want to keep from Robert and Lynn's, and we entertained the children for the afternoon. Later we ate tea at their house after which Debs and Don went to bed, and we returned home to Drumlin. Tomorrow we shall take our belongings up to Claire's parents' house near Inverness and then head south to complete the purchase of our two new properties and organise to have them let. We expect to be away from Drumlin for a couple of weeks.

-oOo-

We arrived back in Yorkshire after a flying visit to Inverness and completed all of our legal affairs in Thirsk on Friday 31st August. We were now the proud owners of two properties which we had to prepare for the letting market. We had arranged to go to my Mum and Dad's house in Scarborough on the afternoon of Saturday 1st September; however, we moved our plans forward by a few hours and set off late morning instead. Claire was driving and I rang to let them know we would be early. There was no reply. I tried again to no avail. We were about two thirds of the way there when I commented to Claire that I thought it was unusual not to be able to reach them, but that they had perhaps gone out shopping in the morning as they were not expecting us to arrive until later. We agreed that this was a reasonable hypothesis when my mobile phone rang. It indicated that the caller was my father. This was not a usual occurrence, if calls had to be made my Mum usually took charge. I knew something was wrong. I answered and immediately could tell from the tone of Dad's voice that Mum had suffered another brain haemorrhage. It had just happened within the last hour and he had just arrived at the hospital. We went straight there.

Almost two years previously to the day in 2010 my mother suffered her first brain haemorrhage which for a time left her very confused, unable to see properly and with limited motor skills. Gradually she recovered and in time her faculties returned. She was an accomplished musician and in great demand as a pianist and organist, indeed our son Martin wanted her to play at his wedding in November 2010. By mid October she had made significant progress, but she was still only able to play relatively simple music if it was in large print due to the damaged caused to the part of her brain that controls vision. Hymn tunes were not a problem, but she was concerned and wanted to be relieved of the obligation to play for the wedding. I remember her calling me to discuss it. I pointed out that in the few months she had been recovering her ability to play had returned quite considerably and that if she continued to improve her abilities would once again be impressive. She could see the logic. I also pointed out that as our family is blessed with more than its fair share of musical talent that if she really was not able to play at the wedding someone else would, but that the whole family wanted HER to do it. She accepted that this was also true. I further pointed out that if I let her off the hook now the imperative to practice and improve would be lost, Martin and the rest of the family would be disappointed that she was not going to play at the wedding, she would give up the chance to shine again, and I was not about to let her throw it all away. It was a hard line to take, but it paid off. She continued to progress and did play for the wedding. In fact she went on to play for a number of performances including the last time I performed with her at the family gathering to celebrate their Golden Wedding. We played my arrangement of "What a Friend We Have in Jesus" and the "Allelujia" from Mozart's Exultate in Jubilate.

The next seven days were a difficult time and by mid week the doctors had told my father that they did not expect her to recover. On the afternoon of Monday 10th September Dad and I were sitting at Mum's bedside when Martin arrived. He came to tell us that he had just had a call from his solicitor to inform him that the contracts had just been exchanged on his first house and he would be able to move in the following week on completion. Martin delivered this news to his grandma in person, news she was eager to receive. She heard it! About half an hour later, with my father, my son and I at her bedside Mum died peacefully.

We had remained in Yorkshire longer than we had intended which allowed us more time to prepare our two new buy-to-let properties for rental, to help our son and daughter in law move into their new house and of course most importantly to support my Dad in the funeral arrangements. It was a busy time.

Chapter Four

Our First Winter

"Cold and damp,- are they not as
rich experience as warmth
and dryness?" [13]
Henry David Thoreau

Thursday 27th September 2012, Troon, Baro 1005, Day 48:
The wind is strong and westerly. We arrived back in Troon at 19.00hrs thanks to a lift by Claire's parents in their car.

Wednesday 3rd October 2012, Troon, Baro 906, Day 54:
We have spent most of the day removing more green algae from the exterior woodwork and applying teak oil. Inside we have damp and wet areas especially in the forepeak. I think some form of duck boards to lift things off the surfaces and to allow air to circulate are required and also perhaps a dehumidifier. More expense, but it will save the boat from too much damage and rot.

Friday 5th October 2012, Troon, Sunny Spells, Day 56:
This morning I went to Ayr by bus to buy a dehumidifier and go to the bank. £6.40 return! (And they wonder why people use their cars!) When I arrived back we turned Drumlin round stern to, so we can reach to clean and teak oil the woodwork along the transom from the pontoons.

Sunday 7th October 2012, Troon, Sunny, Baro 1018, Day 59:
We finished cleaning the woodwork on the port side and it is now ready for teak oiling. We are going to my cousin Robert's for tea tonight and Claire has baked some cakes with icing

on. We dehumidified the forepeak cushions today. After a few weeks of non productivity I managed to write a short "Hosanna" for my Requiem Mass and I began to draft out the "Benedictus". Interestingly during last night I had my first real music withdrawal, dreaming about this composition which prompted me to get on with a bit more!

Monday 8th October 2012, Troon, Cool and Bright, Baro 1018, Day 59:
Most of the woodwork has now been cleaned and at least one coat of teak oil applied. On the downside we ran out of gas just as we began cooking tea, our spare gas bottle is empty and tomorrow the chandlery is shut!

We turned Drumlin back round today using just warps. That went well.

I have been reading up on opera – Not my favourite branch of music, but some revision and extra study will fill in some gaps in my knowledge. It is not good to die ignorant of what you could have learned! Yesterday I revised the life of J S Bach. I have used mind maps for note taking rather than making traditional notes, it is an experiment to see if this strategy works for me.

Thursday 11th October 2012, Troon, Persistent Rain, Baro 1001, Day 62:
I devoted much of today reading about Ballet or watching Thom Bresh (Merle Travis's son) on the guitar playing technique known as Travis picking. A few moments ago I returned from a walk with the dogs and as I paddled through the rain across the marina car park I saw a man climb out of his car wearing a wet suit, and this is no word of a lie, he put a rain coat on to keep dry!

Friday 19th October 2012, Troon, Dull and Occasional Showers, Baro 1006, Day 70:

I spent the morning doing business paperwork and accounts and Claire knitted a waistcoat. In the afternoon we decided that we should buy some 45cm x 45cm wooden decking tiles that we had seen in a local garden centre. These are intended as a quick way of creating a garden decking area, but they are also a perfect and cheap alternative to duck boards, ideal for elevating our bed mattress off the locker lids allowing air to circulate and to keep them off the damp surface. This will be another experiment to see if we can gain the upper hand in the ongoing war on damp.

Saturday 20th October 2012, Troon, Bright, Sometimes Sunny and Cool, Baro 1014, Day 71:

Our experiment with the decking tiles under the bed seems to be working. Last night we enjoyed a warmer mattress and no condensation this morning – The experiment continues...

Monday 22nd October 2012, Troon, Dull and Overcast, Day 73:

Today we deflated and stowed the dinghy, and removed the jack stays from the deck for winter. I went into the quarter berth to check the lockers beneath and to sort the paint and engine spares stored there. The mattress was a little damp so we measured up to work out how many more decking tiles we need to buy to do the same in here as in the forepeak.

Tuesday 23rd October 2012, Troon, Sunny Spells and Cool, Baro 1030, Day 74:

We went into town and I bought some new shoes, some abrasive paper and paint brushes. During the afternoon I made some miniature duck boards to elevate the books on the forepeak bookshelves. I also found more engine spares. We keep unearthing little treasures in Drumlin's various secret crevices as we gradually explore our way around her more intimate parts. We also assembled and prepared all the necessary components necessary to remove the Genoa sail from the roller furling gear.

Other news - My father has seen his consultant for his annual check up following his heart surgery a few years ago and he is happy with his progress. On the down side our son Martin rang today to tell us his pet lizard, a bearded dragon called Phoebe, is at the vet's after quickly becoming ill with a severely depleted blood count. It may be treatable anaemia or it could be leukaemia. How cruelly ironic it is, as today is the twelfth anniversary of Neil's death. Let's hope and pray the poor little creature gets well!

On a positive note, and this should have been logged yesterday, our letting agents called to tell us someone has applied to become a tenant in our second house.

22.15 hrs - I have just listened to Verdi's opera "Un ballo in maschera" (A Masked Ball), a story about the assassination of Gustav III of Sweden Circa 1784. The opera has no real historical truth other than the king was actually killed; the affair with his advisor's wife, which didn't really happen, is purely a dramatic device for the plot. Gustav was actually killed by his politicians who were jealous of the fact that the king had restored order to the country, but also kept much benevolent power for himself.

Wednesday 24th October 2012, Troon, Baro 1028, Day 75:
Our son just rang to tell us that poor Phoebe Lizard died during the night. He is so upset.

Friday 26th October 2012, Troon, Sunny and Cold, Baro 1022, Day 77:
Our son just rang to tell us that the post mortem results showed that Phoebe Lizard did indeed die of leukaemia! There was really no way of knowing before she became ill and little if anything that could have been done for her.

Wednesday 31st October 2012, Troon, 21.00 hrs, Rain, Baro 972, Day 82:
Last night the wind was quite vicious and we didn't sleep very well. Today we have had copious quantities of rain. We have spent a very pleasant day with our friends Norman and Elizabeth who are visiting from Yorkshire.

It is twelve years today that we buried our son Neil.

Today our new tenants moved into our second house and it is finally let. Hurray! The final piece of our plan has been fulfilled.

Thursday 1st November 2012, Troon, Settled Then Winds Rose Mid Afternoon, Baro 970, Day 83:
Today began sunny and calm so we took our visitors Norman and Elizabeth for a 7 mile sail in Irvine Bay. The wind freshened mid afternoon as forecast.

Today Chip, my little terrier, fell in. He decided to jump ashore under the guard rail as I was stepping over it. His lead, which was in my hand, abruptly stemmed his forward motion just as his back legs bade farewell to Drumlin's deck. The result was a half suspended canine up to his armpits in water frantically doggy paddling in two elements, air and water! The score for dunkings now stands at Bracken 2: Chip 1!

Friday 2nd November 2012, Troon, Sunshine and Showers, Baro 978, Day 84:
Today I put some decking tiles / duck boards under the mattress in the quarter berth and some more mini duck boards on the bookshelves, this time the ones in the saloon. The war on damp continues with some degree of success! It was so windy in the night that I got up and put spring shock absorbers onto the mooring lines. They make a significant difference and radically reduce the snatching and shock loads on the cleats.

Sunday 4th November 2012, Troon, Bright and Cold, Baro 998, Day 86:
Jenny and Stewart, my auntie and uncle who live nearby, loaned me their car to go to Scarborough to dispose of my old car which had been recovered from the scene of its untimely demise and parked outside my father's house. It has been sent away for "recycling".

Monday 5th November 2012, Day 87:
I drove the 250 miles to Scarborough and stopped the night at Dad's house.

Tuesday 6th November 2012, Day 88:
I made arrangements with the scrap dealer to remove my old car and made the return 250 mile trip to Drumlin. When I arrived back in Troon Chip was so pleased to see me that he fell in the water and became lodged under the pontoon. It took Claire and I over an hour to rescue him. The score for dunkings stands at Bracken 2: Chip 2!

As I was lifting my bags aboard Drumlin Chip decided to jump off the boat and onto the finger pontoon to greet me. Unfortunately he was too excited, it was fairly dark and he misjudged where the edge of the jetty was resulting in a splash. At this point, if he had swum towards me when I was calling him, I could have reached down and lifted him out of the water, but for some reason it seemed more sensible to him to swim parallel to the jetty just beyond the reach of any potential rescuer in order to seek refuge underneath the planking behind one of the floats. Having located a tiny ledge on which to rest his weary little paws and keep his head just above water his movements stopped, he was out of sight and I had no way of knowing his precise whereabouts. It was at this point I began to think he had gone under. I stood still and listened periodically whistling and calling his name. After a few anxious minutes I heard him just under my feet on the main pontoon. Shining a torch through the gaps in the woodwork positively pinpointed his position. I tried to unscrew the planks, but they were far too well driven home to remove by hand. I then stripped to the waist, and with Claire securing me by the ankles, I edged my way as far over the edge as I could to try to reach under. I could just touch him, but no words of encouragement would persuade him to let go and let me pull him out and in my desperate attempts to free him the concrete and metal structure took the skin off my forearm. The reason I could not get him free soon became clear. The only way out involved a quick dive under the surface to pass by a piece of the pontoon's structure, the piece that was chewing away at my arm. There was only one option left. I had to be in there with him!

Now as much as I love my dog I had no intention of swimming in the sea at night in November, so I had an idea. I inflated the dinghy, launched it, tied it alongside and lay prostrate on the bottom. This allowed me to get a firm grip on his collar with enough free movement in my arm to do the only thing I could. I pulled him down under the water and swiftly up and towards me. Before he could say "Davy Jones Locker", which is "Ger Woof Yelp" in dog, I had hauled him into the dinghy whereupon he showed his eternal gratitude for saving his life by soaking me, shaking himself and leaping out of the boat into Claire's arms. A moment later she rushed him inside, wrapped him in a towel and was drying and warming him up! I soon realised, cold, wet and tired as I was, that I was going to have to fend for myself. I clambered shivering and bleeding out of the dinghy, retrieved my shirt, screwdriver and torch and completed my journey home cold, miserable and wet.

Thursday 8th November 2012, Troon, Day 90:
I put the dinghy away again!

This evening we were invited aboard "Utopie" for supper with her owners Phil and Alison. They are doing the same as us and leaving dry land behind in favour of adventure on the high seas. Like us they have bought a boat from Glasson, intriguingly from the very man I happened to speak to in the chandlery back in July who asked where we were going to take Drumlin. Small world! Unlike us they do not have dogs so they are exchanging their cruising ground of Scotland for the sunnier climes of the Mediterranean. They are a really friendly couple, into folk music, real ale and yachting. Our kind of people! They also shared a very useful anti damp strategy which is to use an electric kettle whenever shore power is available as it uses less gas and causes less condensation.

Friday 9th November 2012, Troon, Windy and Showers, Baro 994, Day 91:
I took Phil and Alison's advice and bought an electric kettle today.

Saturday 10th November 2012, Troon, Breezy and Showers, Day 92:
Today I spent time tidying the cockpit locker and put the outboard motor away. It usually lives on the pushpit, but in winter it is better for it to be inside and protected from the elements. We emptied the quarter berth again to dry it out; damp is still our number one enemy. In the process I discovered a bank of 16 hitherto unknown fuses hidden in one of the quarter berth lockers. Having investigated them we found out that this is where most of the additional electronic and electrical devices are wired and consequently we have fixed the pressurised water system which was temperamental due to a poor fuse connection!

This evening I spent more time working on my Requiem and completed the Agnus Dei.

Sunday 11th November 2012, Troon, Sunny Cool and Calm, Baro 1011, Day 93:
Aired and removed the sails as we will not be requiring them until April next year.

Monday 12th November 2012, Troon, Wet and Windy, Baro 1011, Day 94:
Chip cut his paw when we were out for a walk today resulting in a trip to the vet. No stitches were required, but we think he stood on a shard of glass. I finished writing a Kyrie and Hymnus for my Requiem today and Claire finished knitting another jumper.

Sunday 2nd December 2012, Troon, Sunny, Baro 1015, Day 111:
We stripped everything out of the forepeak to dry it out. Since the introduction of the decking tile duckboards under the mattresses and books everything is staying much drier, but the

walls still run with condensation. The carpet and closed cell foam matting against the sides of the boat are doing a fine job of protecting the bed from getting wet but we still have to keep on top of the damp to prevent rot and mildew. You cannot defy the laws of physics or completely eliminate condensation in this environment, but you can find ways to live with it without suffering from it.

Saturday 29th December 2012, Troon, Wind and Rain, Baro 989, Day 117:
We have just arrived home by train after spending a lovely Christmas with Claire's family near Inverness. The dogs were very well behaved on their first train journey! It is good to be home. Claire's breathing was noticeably worse whilst we have been "indoors". She suffers from chronic asthma and since leaving a brick and mortar environment she has been almost free of symptoms. Drumlin was fine when we returned. A little chafe was evident on one of the mooring lines though. We also noticed that the wind had caused one of the fastenings for the port side dodger to come undone at the forward foot. Her batteries were well charged at 12.4 volts each.

Sunday 30th December 2012, Troon, Very Windy and Rain, Baro 989, Day 118:
We were woken at about half past eight this morning by a very loud bang. The chafed mooring line had snapped. The moral of this story is if it looks chafed, assume it is damaged beyond repair and replace it. Fortunately we had rigged up back up lines so we didn't drift off.

Claire's breathing is improving!

Monday 31st December 2012, Troon, Wind and Rain, Baro 991, Day 119:

Last night we had a force 9 severe gale again. Drumlin copes well with these winds when the shock absorbers are used on her mooring lines so we are not too uncomfortable. It is just noisy.

Well it is now midnight. Happy New Year! We have just arrived back from spending time at my cousin, Robert's house and as midnight struck all the ships in the commercial harbour hooted their horns! Quite extraordinary!

Sunday 6th January 2013, Troon, Wind SW and Rain, Baro 1025, Day 125:

I spent today sitting at home and began work on my first essay. I also readjusted the spray hood.

I had been reading quite a lot of "philosophical" material over the last few years and have been forming some new ideas, at least new to me. I discovered Ralph Waldo Emerson and Henry David Thoreau a few years ago and more recently John Zerzan. Their writings prompted me to explore various subjects and thanks to the internet, and Wikipedia in particular, I have been able to research a lot of topics in a rather random way. Given that the internet is the modern equivalent of a giant encyclopaedia and as such is as reliable or otherwise as its printed counterpart I have treated it as a valid source of information with the caveat that one should always read with a large amount of critical thinking.

Two subjects intrigued me, cynicism in its true philosophical sense and Transcendentalism. I thought it might be an interesting and useful activity for me to try to make some sense of what I had read and learned by taking myself back to school and writing an essay. Consequently I decided to give myself the following statement to discuss:

"Cynicism and Transcendentalism together form a useful philosophy for mental and spiritual health in the modern world."

Monday 7th January 2013, Troon, Wind SE and Rain, Baro 1016, Day 126:
I did the shopping today then we dehumidified the forepeak. We took the books off the shelves and brought them into the saloon and replaced them with washing up bowls containing our clothes. The reasoning behind this is that the bowls will keep the clothes dry and allow air to circulate behind thus reducing the formation of condensation. I WILL beat the damp, AND use the storage space more effectively!

Some books I had ordered to help with my essay arrived today and I also played my guitar this evening. Claire is a bit off colour, not due to my guitar playing, she blames lack of light and sunshine!

Tuesday 8th January 2013, Troon, Wind W Dry and Bright, Baro 1020, Day 127:
We have had a quiet day. We fuelled up with diesel for the central heating and discussed having Drumlin lifted out with the Marina manager.

I also received a reply from the editor of "Practical Boat Owner" in response to my email about using decking tiles under the boat's mattresses to combat damp. My article is to be published in the February 2013 issue!

Friday 11th January 2013, Troon, Cold Easterly and Dull, Baro 1016, Day 130:

I spent the day with my cousin Robert helping him fit out an office at home. Tonight I did for the first time in 30 years some music concrete, experimental electronic music. Unlike in the 1980's I don't now need to use a reel to reel tape recorder and splice pieces of tape together, nowadays a laptop can be used to manipulate the sounds digitally. I made a 9 minute composition using a 2p piece and a pan lid! I have written catchier tunes but this is an event to hear. Not profound, but significant. This is why I made this change to my life; to do this sort of creative stuff.

Sunday 13th January 2013, Troon, Wind S Cold and Wet, Baro 1029, Day 132:

It has been another quiet day inside. I continued reading and also spent time working on some more music concrete. I have determined to compose a suite of 5 x 9 minute symmetrical pieces collectively called "Reflections". They are all inspired by my experience of being reminded at the 2011 Turner Prize Exhibition at the Baltic in Newcastle how I had once been a "modern" composer. This is why we made this life change ... I keep reminding myself!!!

I wrote the following notes to accompany the recordings I made:

In 2011 I visited the BALTIC Centre for Contemporary Arts in Newcastle to see the four works competing for the Turner Prize. One of the artists exhibiting was Hilary Lloyd with her video installation. The other three artists' works were challenging and engaging to me and as I stood in and amongst them I was able, as a non artist, to engage with and internally inquire about them and began to feel a sense of place and immediacy. A classic example of, "You had to be there!" As for Hilary Lloyd's piece, I, like many of those I saw around me, struggled to understand its apparently random moving images on various screens located around the room. It was not until I was in the car going home discussing what we had experienced with my wife that the Lloyd work suddenly made sense to me. As a musician I have a knowledge and appreciation of the medium of sound, as an artist in the broader sense I appreciate, often without any specific "knowledge", the work of other types of artist. It was not until that eureka moment when I made the leap from what I had seen of Lloyd's work to ask the question, "What if she had done that with sound instead of images, how would I have reacted then?" It was at that point that I understood what I had experienced, and to my shame had utterly failed to appreciate at the time. We are so used to hearing a tune in music, but not all music is melody; in Lloyd's work I then felt that I had seen a truly great piece and, in searching for the "melody" failed to see the music in her work. As a consequence I decided at that moment on the A19 travelling south that the 2011 Turner Prize winner should be Hilary Lloyd and knew instantly she would not win. Why? Because in my view she is so far ahead of the rest of us that few would "get" her work, and I suspect that if the judges had, they would have been too afraid of the public's backlash to have selected her.

"What is your point?" I hear you ask. It was in that moment of realisation that I was reminded of my own younger days as a music student; how fired up I was learning about atonal composition, Schönberg and the Second Viennese School, Serial compositional technique, musique concrète, or György Ligeti's "Volumina", John Cage and his prepared piano or Steve Reich's astonishing "Come out to show them". By the 1980s much of this was really out of date and essentially part of musical history and the repertoire part of the emerging canon of modern music. I had learned that music is more than tonality, pretty tunes and a good beat, but I had almost forgotten this! As a consequence of being reminded that I had almost lost sight of where I was originally going on my musical journey, I decided to return to, and devote some of my energy to, exploring and creating new sounds as well as working in the more traditional ways. Although I count myself as a composer of music in these pieces I do not describe them as composed, rather I assembled them from what I found!

-oOo-

Tuesday 16th January 2013, Troon, Wind E Bitterly Cold with Frost, Baro 1009, Day 134:
I finished my essay today. I doubt I would pass an A level with it, but it was fun to do. Five and half thousand words entitled "In Natural Pursuit of Arete". I also assembled piece number 4 of my music concrete suite. Piece number 5 is to be made out of pieces of the other 4 spliced together. Our daughter Hannah rang today to tell me her boyfriend wants to see me! I wonder why?

Tuesday 22nd January 2013, Troon, Wind E Clear Skies and Icy, Baro 1008, Day 141:
I bought the February issue of "Practical Boat Owner" today – Page 59 has my article on beating damp beneath cushions printed word for word! Claire did a large batch of baking and confessed to being homesick last night, not for the house but she is, "Missing the children." The galley sink is blocked again and now the plunger has perished.

Wednesday 23rd January 2013, Troon, Wind E and Dry, Baro 1011, Day 142:

I installed a 60 Watt tube radiator in the forepeak and had to buy a 5 metre extension to plug it in. This is all part of the war on damp. We have not used as much heating oil this week. I have also noticed that the super market were selling cauliflowers before Christmas for 87p, they are now £1 each for the cheap ones. That is a 14.5% increase in price! Outrageous! And whilst I am getting hot under the collar at such blatant profiteering Claire serenely continues to do cross-stitch and to play majong on the laptop.

Nature gave us an instinct

Nature gave us an instinct,
For use when dangers arise,
To act, not having to think,
When caught by fright or surprise.

A response to keep us safe.
They call it "the fight or flight".
Ev'ry member of our race.
Must learn to use it aright.

We won't be chased by tigers.
Nor likely eaten by sharks.
But daily we are hunted.
By those stalked with greedy hearts.

Preys on the population,
Big business, which profit craves.
Sense of self preservation?
Now dull as a blunt knife's blade!

How placidly you give in,
When told, "Please enter your PIN!"
Why questioned never the price?
Spending! Addiction! A vice!

This is the threat we now face.
This is the danger to fight
Stand up, say no and resist.
These predators put to flight.

Let your instinct for living.
Protect you from fiscal harm
Don't be duped into giving
Your wealth for some worthless charm.

Be wary of that bargain
Suspicious of every price?
My friend, begging your pardon,
Take heed of my good advice.

Andrew Dalby, Ardfern, 4th June 2013

-oOo-

Thursday 24th January 2013, Troon, Wind SE Dry and Cold,
Baro 1018, Day 143:
*We emptied the forepeak, cleaned off the beginnings of
mildew, dried and dehumidified. Storing clothes in washing
up bowls is proving to be an effective method of keeping them
away from the condensation, and of letting the walls breathe.
The decking tiles have proved to be most effective against
damp. The new heater made a significant difference to our
comfort during the night and now we shall watch to see how
effective that is in the long term in preventing condensation.*

Friday 25th January 2013, Troon, 18.40 hrs, Wind SE Cold and Rain, Baro 996, Day 144:

I hardly slept last night as I was worrying about our finances. How is it that we cannot seem to spend less than £12 per day in a marina? How will we manage in summer when it is £25 in a marina? As usual I received inspiration in my favourite place, the shower – Rethink the £30 per week idea and aim instead at a £2 per day for food shopping system.

"In proportion as he simplifies his life, the laws of
the universe will appear less complex, and
solitude will not be solitude, nor poverty
poverty, nor weakness weakness." [14]
Henry David Thoreau

Today I also spoke to our letting agents about buying another investment property in the same area as one we already have. They are confident it is not a bad idea as they have another landlord with 5 houses in the same street.

Saturday 26th January 2013, Troon, Wind Strong SW Cold and Rain, Baro 978, Day 145:

During the night the wind veered NW, was quite strong and then settled to the SE during the day. Gales are forecast. We quietly worked through the day emptying the port side lookers in the saloon and drying them out. We shall use the washing up bowl strategy in these lockers too as a means to protect the contents from damp. This evening we watched a couple of films on DVD which took my mind off things. I seem to have suddenly lost perspective and confidence in what we are doing. My demons are threatening to return!

Depression

There you are, just minding your own business,
Then there it is!
It just sneaks up on you.
One minute you're fine then the next you're wrapped in it,
Like a cold wet blanket!
That chilly feeling of hopelessness!
That clammy sensation of dread!
Like a cloud blocks out the sunlight
And sheds its cargo of rain,
So comes the demon,
The courier of my pain.

Andrew Dalby, Thirsk, 26th May 2009

Anyone who has experienced clinical depression may recognise the symptoms when, or if, they recur. As a serial sufferer of the condition this poem marks the onset of a period of illness accompanied by a period of increased creativity. (I am usually at my most creative when depressed.) What was unusual about this particular episode (in 2009) was the fact that the creativity was more poetic than musical. Some of my underlying conflicts found a voice, and themes that I had previously tried to deny or suppress, or which were thinly disguised or hidden from my conscious began to emerge clearly and distinctly.

-oOo-

Sunday 27th January 2013, Troon, Strong W Showers, Baro 982, Day 146:
We emptied the quarter berth today to dry, clean and dehumidify it. There was some condensation but not very

much. A victory against the old enemy damp! I have been thinking about this low point that I have reached; about the same amount of time (4 – 5 months) has elapsed since my Mum died as did after Neil died and I hit a low then too. I wonder if this is significant?

This strong wind is forecast to stay with us for a while, not very encouraging.

Monday 28th January 2013, Troon, S10 Rain, Baro 977, Day 147:
It was decided today that I should go to Yorkshire by train to investigate the purchase of a third property and to make any necessary arrangements if the house we had been watching on the internet is suitable. We also took the spray hood down before the severe winds damaged it.

My trip south proved to be very successful and by the 4th February we had our finances arranged and our offer on the third house had been accepted subject to survey. I returned to Troon on the 6th February.

The British parliament has been debating recently whether to legalise gay marriage and it seemed to me unfortunate that the gay community, having made huge leaps forward in being accepted in society, wants to seek the blessing of its former oppressors the Church and State! It is not that I do not wish them to have what they want, they should have the same rights as everyone else, but as I have it (marriage) and have come to realise that it is one of civilisation's many repressive institutions it seems strange to me that they should feel so strongly desirous of it!

On Gay Marriage

So, you want to get married!
To join in matrimony,
In a legal contract,
So everyone can see.

You think that this should be your right,
To enter this estate,
You want the freedom granted all
To raise a prison gate!

For many years the law declared,
The love they dared not name
Was wholly unacceptable,
Illegal, and a shame.

You've been for most of hist'ry,
Despised, outcast, oppressed.
And now you want to join us all,
To be just like the rest!

For me this aim just makes no sense,
For this, your precious goal,
Was by Church and state designed,
A form of social control.

Having loosed the bonds of law,
And turned the tide of hate,
Why do you want to enter in
Another oppressèd state?

It was because you're different
That you suffered sore,
And now you're free to go your way.

Why let them harm you more?

It's not a piece of paper.
It's not a business deal.
Marriage is a state of mind,
And love, its bond and seal.

Try to see beyond the lie,
This civilised institution,
Is not a blessing from God on high,
It's a means of retribution.

Blaze a trail to pastures new,
Find a fresh and novel way,
And show the world a better life,
Than that we have today.

So don't aspire to copy those
Who, for centuries, you denied,
Lead the way to a better place,
Where, happier, we'll all reside.

Andrew Dalby, Troon, 10th February 2013

-oOo-

Thursday 14th February 2013, Troon, W5 Showers, Baro 1009, Day 164:
We started preparing in earnest for the new season by doing an engine oil change and fitting a new oil filter. The job was not as messy as I had envisaged thankfully. (The engine is effectively accessed via a panel in the saloon. It is rather like servicing the car in the living room. Not ideal!)

Thursday 21st February 2013, Troon, SE Cold and Bright, Baro 1026, Day 171:
I changed the fuel filter today and ran the engine for 30 minutes to make sure there were no air locks in the fuel system.

Friday 22nd February 2013, Troon, SE Cold and Overcast, Baro 1029, Day 172:
We visited the Chandlery today to price up the equipment we need for the coming season. We also received a disappointing e-mail from the company who took our life raft away to service it. They say that due to its age and lack of proper servicing in the past it is unserviceable and needs to be written off. I am not pleased!

TAX

T.
A.
X.

T
Apostrophe
X

T'ax. What
A Yorkshireman uses to fell an
"X" mas tree.

T. A. Spells Ta.
A word for thanks, and
X, what your teacher put if an answer was wrong.

They. Them. The Government.

Always asking, grasping, rasping away, and we
Xanthos yellow cowardly comply.

Tax, tacks, nails, sails, zigzag, and they, like an
Algerian pirate, tack towards us, tack and track us down with
their three mast
Xebec of T, A and X.

Ta. They thank us
Always asking, grasping, rasping away, we grant them the
Xenium tribute they don't deserve.

Thus like slaves we meekly comply,
And offer up what's ours by right
Xeransis dry we're bled.

Ta, X. Thanks. Wrong. Tax is wrong.
A man, finds it binds and grinds, it claws for more this
Xantho crab, xenium eating, xeransis bleeding, xebec sailing,
always asking, grasping, rasping, nailing, tacking, taxing, tax.

Andrew Dalby, Troon, 22nd February 2013

There has been much discussion in the news recently about
taxation and several things worry me profoundly about it.
Firstly the propaganda pedalled by the media is that there is a
moral dimension to paying tax and that finding legitimate
ways not to is wrong. In my view this is simply not true. You
should only pay for what you use and not be forced to buy or
contribute to what you do not want, or agree with. Secondly,
to justify the punitive taxation of the masses to pay for the
folly of political and financial institutions, they need to divert
our attention and encourage the resentment of the wealthy and
wealth creators. What our government refuses to see is that
they and the general population would be better off if money

is allowed to flow in the economy, thus allowing for the creation of jobs, the generation of wealth and consequently the collection of reasonable and affordable, even dare I say it some justified taxation!

"But the state tells lies in all the tongues
of good and evil; and whatever
it says it lies – and whatever
it has it has stolen." [15]
Nietzsche

Saturday 23rd February 2013, Troon, NE Sunny, Baro 1030, Day 173:
We took the dogs for a really long walk today and Claire is stitching together a knitted triangular blanket for our bed in the forepeak to keep us warm now spring is coming! I have written some more poetry this time raging against taxation and deforestation. Easy bedtime reading! To relax this evening we watched a film.

Killing The Trees

Another lorry, another load, another wagon comes down the road,
A hundred living impressive trees, felled by the axe man below the knees,
To fuel a machine that's never slowed, and killing the trees no mercy showed.

A crane grabs the logs, hauls them up high, swinging them over, piled high and stowed,
Into the roller, frightful and dark, gnawed by the molars, chewed off, the bark.

Another lorry, another load, another wagon comes down the
road!

Three decades growing, two feet per year, sap freely flowing
from sapling sowed;
Into the sawmill, naked and bare, hacked into pieces, no one
to care,
To fuel a machine that's never slowed, and killing the trees no
mercy showed.

Packed into bundles, stamped with a code, picked up by fork
lift, another load,
Mountains of sawdust, drumlins of bark, when will this wood
lust loose all its spark?
Another lorry, another load, another wagon comes down the
road,

Another lorry, another load, another journey, another woe?
Where will they take it, what will it be, will it be valued, will
it used, be
To fuel a machine that's never slowed? And killing the trees
no mercy showed.

How will it finish, where will it end, what will become of our
forest friend?
When will eyes open to see the trend, when will men wake up
and trees defend?
Another lorry, another load, another wagon comes down the
road,
To fuel a machine that's never slowed, and killing the trees no
mercy showed.

Andrew Dalby, Troon, 23rd February 2013

When I wrote this poem, just down the road from where I was living, opposite Troon harbour is a large wood processing plant, a sawmill. Logs are brought in by lorry and they are transformed into planks of timber. If each lorry carries let's say 50 trees that have grown at a rate of 2 feet per year for 30 years, that is 1500 years of tree growth per lorry load. If the factory only took 4 lorry loads per day for 5 days a week, that is 1000 trees per week and 30000 years of growth. If the factory is in production for 48 weeks in the year it will use 48000 trees or 1 million 440 thousand years of growth. This is just one of many such factories around the world. Who can honestly say that we can plant enough trees to keep this up?

"To sin against the earth is now the
most dreadful thing, ..." [16]
Nietzsche

-oOo-

Sunday 24th February 2013, Troon, Calm and Sunny, Baro 1036, Day 174:
We changed the engine's impellor today, the piece of the engine that pumps cold water around the engine to stop it getting too hot. We also changed the alternator drive belt.

Tuesday 26th February 2013, Troon, Sunny, Baro 1039, Day 176:
We received a number of legal papers to check through concerning the purchase of our third house and confirmation the financing is all on track. I also managed to get a little varnishing done around the companionway.

Wednesday 25th February 2013, Troon, Fog, Baro 1039, Day 177:

A number of telephone calls have been made and received concerning the progress of the house purchase. The survey has come back giving the house a clean bill of health and the vendor wants to complete on 28th March which suits us well.

All of the necessary engine spares have now been bought and brought aboard.

Thursday 28th February 2013, Troon, W1, Baro 1039, Day 178:

Pope Benedict XVI (Joseph Aloisius Ratzinger) resigns tonight having served as pope since 19 April 2005 following the death of Pope John Paul II. Apparently he is the first pope to relinquish office of his own accord since 1294 when Pope Celestine V did. His is also the only pope to resign since Pope Gregory XII in 1415, but he was forced to step down to put an end to a row which divided the Catholic Church when it had several men claiming the role! Historically this debacle is known as the Western Schism.

Other news - I fished a log out of the fairway and rubbed down some of the flaking nonslip deck paint ready for painting. It has been the first day this year that has been warm and sunny enough to sit out in the cockpit for most of the day.

Depression Forecast!

Another low approaches, dark clouds overhead,
Weather forecast for my brain, rain will fall again,
Feelings of guilt engulf me, shame and sense of dread.

When I was a little boy, naughty, sent to bed,
Tiree, Lerwick, Malin Head, shipping forecast said,
Another low approaches, dark clouds overhead!

Didn't know what I had done, what it was I'd said,
Pressure rising, sea state slight, soon it will be night,
Feelings of guilt engulf me, shame and sense of dread.

That same emotion here now, heavy heart like lead,
Dogger, Humber, German bight, land is out of sight,
Another low approaches, dark clouds overhead!

This is what it's like for me, this the path I tread,
Dover, Portland, Shannon, Sole, soon to take their toll,
Feelings of guilt engulf me, shame and sense of dread.

The slightest thing can start it, tiny silly things,
There's nothing can prevent it! Waiting in the wings
Another low approaches, dark clouds overhead,
Feelings of guilt engulf me, shame and sense of dread.

Andrew Dalby, Troon, 2nd March 2013

This is a poem about my experience of the first warning signs of depression. It would lend itself well to performance by three voices, the subject, a narrator and the forecast broadcaster. I was prompted to write it because my son telephoned me late last night (1st March) from his home two hundred miles away to tell me his pet cockatiel was unwell.

After the call I was left feeling helpless, useless and worried because of my inability to assist either my son or his pet! This is a typical, relatively minor "knock" that can initiate in me the tell tale symptoms of depression. It is not the severity of the knock itself as much as the timing which is significant. My vulnerability to a depressive episode can sneak up on me without me realising, and it is the nudge from such a minor event that triggers the irrationally disproportionate feelings. I have experienced this effect so many times over the years that I can now usually recognise them for the warning that they are, and I can normally take appropriate actions to defend myself against them. I have tried to describe the feelings as similar to those we experience as children when we have been naughty, but these worthless adult feelings come without a real cause to blame them on. They exist on their own!

My son's pet bird had recovered by the following day.

-oOo-

FENCED IN

Fractured, Every Nook, Cockaigne's expancE!

Exclusion! Division! Since Noah's arC!

Nature looted, polluted, hoarded wheN

Civilisation's leaders bleed it, takE

Ev'rything. Creation's 'Nnihilation! Edging ofF.

Andrew Dalby, Troon, 3rd March 2013

The ultimate symbol of civilisation is the fence. Since hunter-gatherers first settled the land, domesticated animals, invented the idea of property, law, tribute and tax; since mankind left his natural state, divided labour, invented class systems, embraced violence and war and imposed state and religion on our species, the fence has been the method of division, of separation, the means of segregating the strong from the weak, the rich from the poor and the tool that the few use to dominate the many. If we are to rebel, to return to our natural state, the first things that should go are the fences!

> "The relative wholeness of pre-civilised life was first
> and foremost an absence of the narrowing,
> confining separation of people into
> differentiated roles and
> functions." [17]
> John Zerzan

-oOo-

Monday 4th March 2013, Troon, SE-W Sunny Spells, Baro 1015, Day 182:
Drumlin was lifted out of the water today and placed on the hard overlooking the Clyde Cruising Club moorings. Claire cleaned the hull top sides and I painted the hull with antifouling paint. The hull's condition was very good and only required the power hose to pressure wash off the slime. The paint was sound and not flaking. By 5.30 pm I had finished!

This is a rather precarious position to sleep for the night. Drumlin has a gentle slope backwards and is sitting about 6 feet from the 30 feet drop into the marina! The stern is supported by a couple of posts and the bows by one. We are in fact much more secure and safe than we feel! As for the dogs they are back to being hoisted up and down a ladder.

We shall try to finish the work tomorrow and have Drumlin re-launched as soon as possible.

Tuesday 5th March 2013, Troon, SE1 Sunny and Cold, Baro 1006, Day 183:
I applied another coat of antifouling today as I had quite a lot left. We also put teak oil on the woodwork along the stern. We also received the contracts to sign ready for the purchase of the house.

Wednesday 6th March 2013, Troon, E Cold and Rain at Times, Baro 1003, Day 184:
Drumlin was re-launched today.

Monday 11th March 2013, Troon, NE Sunny, Baro 1021, Day 189:
The wind is still very cold and the temperature has not risen above 0°C, and we have had a few more flurries of snow. The wind dropped in the early evening and it has become a still and clear night. It is going to be cold one.

I bought 10 metres of anchor chain for our second anchor. I also bought the Admiralty charts for the Mull of Kintyre to Ardnamurchan Point and some netting to put along the guard rails to stop the dogs from falling overboard. We are nearly ready for setting off now.

Wednesday 13th March 2013, Troon, E Sunny, Baro 1017, Day 191:
We washed the mainsail and bent it onto the boom and hoisted the genoa and attached the sheets. The main sheet was rather dirty so we gave it a soak in a mild solution of bleach

which seems to have done the trick. The topping lift is very perished and needs replacing before we sail. I also managed to add another coat of teak oil to the rubbing strip and toe rails and Drumlin is beginning to look smart again.

All in all it has been a productive day.

Wednesday 27th March 2013, Troon, Wind E3 Sunny and Snow Showers, Baro 1021, Day 205:
I painted some of the deck paint at the rear of the boat. Claire aired the forepeak. This afternoon we bought 2 x 25litre water carriers and a new quilt for the bed. Our solicitor rang to say we exchanged contracts on the house today.

Thursday 28th March 2013, Troon, E2 Cold and Sunny, Baro 1021, Day 206:
I did some more deck painting and bought some new rope for the topping lift and danbuoy. We fitted the new ropes and found the topping lift easier to do than we had anticipated as it involved sewing the new rope onto the end of the old one and pulling it up the mast, through the sheave down the interior of the mast and out at the bottom. What could possibly have gone wrong? Claire repaired the stitching on the dodgers ready for them to be refitted.

Having exchanged contracts yesterday we completed the purchase of the house today at 1pm and our letting agents already have prospective tenants lined up to view the property.

Sunday 31st March 2013, Troon, SE5 Sunny, Baro 1017, Day 209:
Our son Martin is visiting us; it is Easter Sunday and his 26th birthday today. We went for a shakedown sail and covered 10 nautical miles and made good speed. Drumlin behaved herself

impeccably and all of her gear worked well. This evening we went out for a meal at the local hotel as a treat for Martin's birthday.

Monday 1st April 2013, Troon, SE4 Fair, Baro 1020, Day 210: *Martin returned home today. It was lovely having him aboard, he is a fine young man and we are very proud of him. Claire and I provisioned the boat ready for departure hopefully tomorrow after we pay our dues at the Marina.*

Portpatrick

Glenarm

Carrickfergus Castle

Port Ellen, Islay

Gigha

Craignish Lagoon

Port Ramsay

Coll

Chapter Five

Theory into Practice

"...the poet turns the world into glass, and
shows us all things in their right
series and procession." [18]
Ralph Waldo Emerson

Tuesday 2nd April 2013, Blackfarland Bay, Wind E Dry and
Cold, Baro 1027, Day 211:
*We set sail from Troon at lunchtime intending to go to Buck
Bay in Loch Fyne. Initially the winds were very light so by the
time we had reached the southern end of the Isle of Bute we
were behind time and likely to run out of daylight for
anchoring. We opted to head for Blackfarland Bay opposite
Tighnabruaich instead. The easterly wind picked up slightly
and we made a steady 4 to 5 knots until we were about 2 miles
from our destination when it dropped again, so we motored to
the bay, dropped anchor and had our dinner before settling
for the night.*

Free Night 9

Wednesday 3rd April 2013, Blackfarland Bay, ENE3-4 Sunny,
Baro 1030, Day 212:
*We spent the day chilling, initially literally as it began very
cold, eventually the sun came out and warmed us up where we
were, which was sheltered from the wind. The leisure battery
cannot cope with having the anchor light on all night. I think
it is worn out. 10 hours of a light drawing 0.8 amps should
not drain an 110A.h. battery. As a backup we deployed our
garden solar lamp bought for £1 in the local bargain shop.
Perhaps we do not comply with the International Regulations*

for the Prevention of Collisions at Sea, but it is better than nothing in a crisis! First thing this morning we re-anchored a little closer to the shore in shallower water.

Free Night 10

Thursday 4th April 2013, Blackfarland Bay, NE3 Fair and Some Sun, Baro 1027, Day 213:
I think the leisure battery is to all intents and purposes dead. I have tested it and experimented with it, but does not hold any charge! The garden lamps were quite bright as back up anchor lights.

Free Night 11

Saturday 6th April 2013, Blackfarland Bay, 15.25 hrs, S variable Overcast, Baro 1029, Day 215:
What a day so far! It is about 15.25 hrs and I have just received a phone call. It was quite amazing to hear a very familiar Northern Irish voice but through quite the wrong medium. Every day we listen to the Belfast Coastguard weather broadcasts, and the voice on the phone belonged to one of the people who broadcast them. The lady coastguard wanted to know if we are okay. Apparently we have been spotted by a "concerned" local. We have been anchored here four nights and we do move about the deck, but someone across the loch has identified us and reported our presence. At least it proves that the CG66 scheme that yachts can subscribe to giving the coastguard the vessel's details works as a means of monitoring safety at sea. Personally I think its mischief on the part of the "member of the public" who reported us. We were probably spoiling their view! If Drumlin did not have her name emblazoned along her dodgers the person reporting would not have been able to provide the authorities with any clue as to our identity. I doubt they would have taken any trouble otherwise!

Free Night 13

As I understand it a Haiku poem is 3 lines long 5, 7 and 5 syllables respectively, and it contains two ideas separated by a "cutting" word and a seasonal reference. Today I tried my first one.

Blackfarland

Blackfarland, West Bute,
Looking at Tighnabruaich,
Cut off by north wind.

Andrew Dalby, Tighnabruaich, 4th April 2013

The Moon

Some say the moon is made of cheese,
A lunar Gorgonzola,
A great round disk of milk and whey,
The night sky's glowing roller.

I say, a pancake is the moon,
A circle, pocked and cratered,
Flour, eggs and milk all mixed with spoon,
In pan, fried, tossed, then plated.

So say, when up at night you look,
And the moon, she holds your gaze,
I cannot shrink you, astral dish,
To a snack on which to graze.

Andrew Dalby, Tighnabruaich, 5th April 2013

-oOo-

Sunday 7th April 2013, Bagh Buic, S–SE2, Baro 1020, Day 216:

We relocated to Loch Fyne. It was a pleasant motor and sail to get here. We are not sure how good the holding will be and the wind is forecast to increase so we shall have to set an anchor watch tonight. I just saw a seal as I was writing!

Free Night 14

Monday 8th April 2013, Bagh Buic, SE5 , Baro 1009, Day 217:

We have remained in this bay after a rather windy night. At first as the wind rose the anchor dragged, but then set itself and we stayed put through the rest of the night. I think there is a bed of weed that initially made the anchor slip then it dug into the sand.

Margaret Thatcher – the former UK Prime Minister died this morning aged 87 in London.

Free Night 15

Tuesday 9th April 2013, Black Harbour, SE< 5, Baro 1009, Day 218:

Bagh Buic was rather bumpy last night so we decided to come into Black Harbour. It is much quieter in here and more sheltered. We tandem anchored in 9m of water and so far we are holding very fast. Dad rang today to say that he is coming up to Troon today and stopping at my Auntie's caravan. Tomorrow we shall head back to Troon to see him.

This bay is full of seals; so far I have counted 12 on the islet opposite not including those swimming around us.

Other news - It has been announced that Mrs Thatcher's funeral will take place a week tomorrow, Wednesday 17th April.

Free Night 16

Wednesday 10th April 2013, Troon, SE2-4 Misty with Sunny Spells, Day 219:

We enjoyed a calm and quiet night in Black Harbour which turns out to be a good shelter from easterly winds. At 12.30 we set off for Troon, typically the wind was SE and therefore right on the nose as far as the bottom end of the Cowal peninsular then when we arrived there it dropped completely. We were left motoring into a very calm and still sea. As evening approached and we were passing West Kilbride the wind began to pick up again, but we still had to motor all the way back to Troon. We arrived at 20.30hrs. It was actually a really pleasant journey.

As always it was a great pleasure to have my father with us between 11th and 13th April but sadly the weather was not sailing weather. Between the 14th and 18th April we were quite literally trapped in Troon, pinned down by southerly gales and unable to go anywhere because the weather was simply too dangerous to venture out. On a positive note however the air was warmer due to the southerly component in the wind. The barometer began to rise, and by Thursday 18th was 1009 and the wind had veered from south to North West. Predictably the very direction we wanted to head in to get to Rothesay!

Wednesday 17th April 2013, Troon, Torrential Rain then Dull and Overcast, Baro 1004 / 988, Day 226:

We had a fairly calm night, but as the day progressed the wind picked up and by this evening was blowing force 8 again! The weather reports forecast more of the same for tomorrow.

We listened to Mrs Thatcher's funeral and thanks to the wonders of the internet we managed to see some pictures of the event too. Whatever one may think of her as a politician one cannot deny that she has certainly made her mark in history.

Friday 19th April 2013, Rothesay, Variable <3 but Mainly SW, Baro 1030, Day 228:

We left Troon at midday and sailed and motored to Rothesay. It is always tricky in variable winds to keep sailing in one direction when the wind is dancing around in every direction like a puppy asking you to throw a stick, but it has been a beautiful if rather chilly day. On arrival we anchored just off the sailing club using both anchors in tandem in a bid to ensure better holding. I think we could need it as my father rang from Scarborough today to tell us his fence has blown down!

Free Night 17

Saturday 20th April 2013, Rothesay, S4-5, Baro 1028, Day 229:

There is a lot of history in Rothesay, in particular a rather magnificent round castle surrounded by a moat. It has been the scene of some rather unsavoury battles. In the year 1230 the Vikings took the castle, but they failed to keep possession of it for long. Again in 1263 King Haakon IV took it again from King Alexander III, but after the battle of Largs he lost it again. This was effectively the end of Viking rule in Scotland, but to be fair they hung on nearly 200 years longer than they did in England if you don't count William the Conqueror as an expat Viking!

We enjoyed a calm night last night and have remained at anchor all day, but the wind has been freshening throughout the day and is forecast to be gusting force 7 during the night.

The bay has been busy all day with the usual ferries, some tug boats working and a Royal Navy ship passed through.

Free Night 18

Tuesday 23rd April 2013, Rothesay, Variable 3-4, Baro 1017, Day 232:

This morning a curious thing happened. Whilst I was on the foredeck fishing a Police vessel left the harbour, but sauntered past us, when I paid attention to it by eyeballing them they quickly made off as if they had been caught prying. I mentioned this to Claire and we both suspected that "concerned" of Bute was perhaps reporting our presence just like the incident in Blackfarland Bay when the coast guard rang us up. Call me paranoid if you want to, and maybe I am!

Other news - I painted a little more of the deck with nonslip paint, at lunch time an Ocean Youth trust yacht anchored next to us briefly, and the leisure battery serving the 12v electrical system is dead. RIP battery. More expense!

Free Night 21

Wednesday 24th April 2013, Rothesay, W to NW4, Baro 1022, Day 233:

This morning at about 08.50 hrs I was on deck taking down the Anchor light and checking the security of the anchor ball when Claire alerted me to another strange occurrence. Overlooking the bay by the Sailing Club in a place not normally used for the parking of cars was a police car. Claire said that she thought we were, "Being watched". No sooner had she said this than I noticed the third strange event in this episode. At that moment a motor vessel departed the harbour and was heading at speed directly towards us. This is not a usual direction for boats to travel when leaving the harbour. A minute later the Harbour Master was alongside enquiring if we were okay because someone hadn't noticed any activity on our boat! I pointed out that I had spent some time on deck both painting and fishing during the last few days, not to mention the dogs on their hourly comfort patrols. He seemed satisfied and left.

Other news - I rowed ashore to walk the dogs and do some shopping.

Free Night 22

Thursday 25th April 2013, Innellan Bay, W5, Baro 1023, Day 234:

Today we motored round Toward point to the little anchorage known as Innellan Bay which is opposite Wemyss (Pronounced "Weems") Bay where the ferries from the mainland to Bute depart. We wanted a change of scenery. Innellan is a good place for a view of the Clyde and the prolific amount of traffic entering and departing Glasgow and her associated ports. On the down side this little bay is rather prone to swell and the effects of wakes from passing vessels so it was rather bouncy. Our anchor held well in spite of a couple of classic squalls with their sudden wind shifts and violent gusts of wind and rain.

Free Night 23

Friday 26th April 2013, Millport, NW6-7, Baro 1016, Day 235:

We decided that a move to Great Cumbrae would be a good idea in the light of the fact that Northerly winds are forecast. We aimed for Millport which lies sheltered on the southern edge of Great Cumbrae via the Largs channel intending to check out a little anchorage called Balloch Martin that a friend had alerted us to, half way down the east side of the island. We found the anchorage, but as the wind was lively decided to continue to Millport. At this point the wind had not yet completely veered to the north. On rounding the Hunterston 9 Port Hand Channel Marker buoy Millport came into view and looked distinctly uninviting as it was being thoroughly strafed by the wind. We decided that we would return to Ballock Martin and anchored there for a few hours. Given the strength of the wind this sweet little anchorage was rather bumpy and we could not get the anchor to hold reliably so at tea time we weighed and returned round the corner to Millport where at least we knew we would be on solid and well maintained moorings. By this time the wind had also come round to the north.

This evening we have enjoyed the entertainment provided by the seals on the island opposite.

Free Night 24

Saturday 27th April 2013, Millport, N3-4 Sunny, Baro 1022, Day 236:

We went ashore and had fish and chips from "The Deep Sea" fish shop on the front. Claire likes mushy peas with her fish and chips, something not usually available in Scotland, and when I asked the Turkish proprietor for some he immediately said, "Ah, you are from Yorkshire!" Of course he was correct and I enquired as to how he had arrived at this conclusion. He informed me that he had trained and worked in Yorkshire for 10 years, in fact he had worked at the "Wetherby Whaler" fish restaurant on Clifton Moor in York. A place we have dined a number of times in the past. This meal may in fact not have been the first one he had ever made for us!

Free Night 25

Sunday 28th April 2013, Troon, W5–8 Squally Showers, Baro 1007, Day 237:

We were woken by the swift arrival of a south westerly storm at half past midnight which took several hours to lessen. We got up at 7.30am and had a good breakfast before setting off for Troon. The squalls were very strong and the sea moderate to rough. We arrived back in Troon shortly after lunch just in time to avoid a significant increase in wind strength and a deluge of rain.

Monday 29th April 2013, Troon, NW5-7 Sunny, Baro 1016, Day 238:

We both slept well after the previous night in Millport and we awoke to a beautiful but windy day. We bought a new leisure battery and I tested the electrical system each device at a time to ascertain how many amps each one uses. I was amazed to find that the LPG gas alarm uses 0.3amps an hour. That is 8 amps per day! Little wonder the battery keeps going flat. Needless to say we have disconnected it, as it has no on/off switch, and have to be VERY careful to turn the gas off when we are not using it.

Tuesday 30th April 2013, Kings Cross Point Lamlash Bay, 22.05 hrs, SW, Baro 1029, Day 239:

We have gone feral again! We left Troon after lunch and fought against a SW wind as we ventured westwards to Arran. We have often visited this bay over the years, but we have never anchored here. We tandem anchored in 8m of water near the fish farm. It is calm and settled in here although we can see the wind's effects above us as it tumbles over the top of the island. Tonight is the first trial of our new battery. The mast head all round white anchor light is on. Tomorrow we shall see how much power has been consumed. It has been a very pleasant day with sunshine and relative warmth.

Free Night 26

Have You Got The Time?

Oft heard the question, "Have you got the time?"
A singular specific ask is this!
As if it is a treasure lost to find,
A hoard of riches we would all possess.

Oft made the comment, "Died before his/her time."
And, though we know not when our lives will end,

We gladly sell our hours in daily grind
To use what little time is left, to spend!

Oft times we sit while minutes pass us by.
Time wasted, squandered, while we rest or play,
And guilty made to feel are we, who try
To savour each free moment of our day.

But time is ours, is here, is now and known
To all who care to "Make the time" they own!

Andrew Dalby, Lamlash, 2nd May 2013

We are now out of Troon Marina and cruising from place to place and I am often very aware of how other people continue to work and live routine lives; like the one I had. It is tempting to allow feelings of guilt enter one's consciousness. Am I unworthy of the leisure time I enjoy? Should I be working and productive? Am I just lazy and is this way of life a waste of time and talent? Assuming the abilities I have can be regarded as talent, how best should I use them?

I have taught music all my life, yet I am equally capable of performing, but this I have done relatively little and for no real financial reward! I can also compose music, but until now I have had little time to, but now I can, and do for its own sake and not to meet the need for some group or performance.

I also write poems, and these are a vehicle through which I express beliefs, ideas and thoughts. They are perhaps worthy in their own right if anyone should choose to read or hear them and the views and sentiments they contain.

This question of time arises from a conflict within our brainwashed minds that holds the assumption that work and labour are good and that leisure time is a benevolent gift graciously bestowed on those who deserve it. Nonsense! Because of the oppressive society we live in and the lack of freedom we enjoy to live our lives as we want, many people become trapped in a cycle of work to meet the demands imposed on them by the system. Our time IS our own. Civilisation would take it from us for a small price they call a wage, then it asks us to pay the money back in order to buy what we need to survive in their system. I say, "Reclaim your time, reclaim your life!"

-oOo-

Friday 3rd May 2013, Kings Cross Point Lamlash, SW5 Persistent Rain, Baro 1007, Day 242:
Kings Cross Point is the southern end of a crescent shape on the eastern side of Arran. In front of this bay is another smaller island called Holy Isle. According to Hamish Haswell-Smith's excellent book "The Scottish Islands" Holy Isle got its name in 1830 when the Arran village at the northern end of this bay took the name Lamlash for itself. Lamlash is a corruption of Saint Mo Las who was an Irish saint born around the year AD566 and who lived on the island in a cave. Legend has it that he lived until he was 120 years old. The cave also has runic early Christian inscriptions some of which date from Haakon's fleet which visited here in AD1263. In AD 1548 the 5 year old Mary Queen of Scots ship sheltered here when she was en route to France. This bay was also a fleet anchorage for the Royal Navy during the First World War.

The rain has been torrential today putting an end to my attempt to go ashore with the dogs. Having inflated the dinghy this morning the heavens opened filling it with 2 inches of water so Claire made shortbread and I planned for our next passage to Campbeltown.

Free Night 29

Saturday 4th May 2013, Campbeltown, SW then W5-6, Baro 1012, Day 243:

We decided to come to Campbeltown today as the wind was forecast to blow from the south or southwest and there was to be little rain. Typically the wind was just slightly too south west to sail so we had to motor all the way. If I'd wanted a motor boat I would have bought one! I can also say, having just heard from Claire's family in Dingwall just north of Inverness that there is snow (In May!), that I can think of little to commend Scotland as a place to sail.

We are anchored in the south eastern part of Campbeltown Loch in 7m – 10m of water. All the chain is out, the wind is blowing and we seem to be holding. We have only put out one anchor with a tripping line.

Free Night 30

I should perhaps confess to becoming a little irascible of late; Claire might say downright miserable to be with, but being a Yorkshireman to my core, the definition of which has been described as a Scotsman with the generosity removed, I have been feeling the pain of being parted from my cash. I blame the weather for this! It is not the case that the wind has not been blowing; it has simply been blowing in the wrong direction. I know that in cruising circles they say that if you are sailing into wind you are going the wrong way, but to be fair it has seemed that whatever the direction we choose to point Drumlin the wind will, like a recalcitrant teenager as a matter of principle, blow from that direction. Having bought sails to be fuelled by the wind it grieves me sorely to have to pay for diesel! In the interest of balance I should also say, as I am writing this after the fact and in a better frame of mind, that Scotland is a very good place to sail, often!

-oOo-

Sunday 5th May 2013, Campbeltown, S3 fair and quite warm, Baro 1014, Day 244:

This morning was spent planning the passage from here to Glenarm in Northern Ireland for each day between now and Thursday 9th May. If we can get a NW or SE wind, not too strong, in a slight sea and good weather we will go.

This afternoon we heard a cuckoo! Make of that what you will...

Free Night 31

Monday 6th May 2013, Campbeltown, SE5 Sunny Spells, Baro 1016, Day 245:

During the night the anchor chain seemed to grind a lot and despite the wind we were lying at an unusual angle to the tripping line buoy which marks where the anchor is. At 4.30 am we concluded that the explanation was that the anchor chain was fouled. Basically we were further east than we should have been and consequently we had wrapped our chain around a wreck. I figured out that the way we were lying and the position of the tripping line suggested that we were wrapped clockwise around the obstacle so we carefully unwound ourselves, weighed the anchor and relocated a little further to the west; just as we were finishing the wind and rain arrived again.

Lesson learned? Double check that you are exactly where you think you are and never assume anything.

I subsequently looked at the charts and compared the position of the wreck with information on the Royal Commission on the Ancient and Historical Monuments of Scotland website. The charts seem to be rather approximate in the position of the wreck. The website also tells us that the unfortunate vessel was a steam yacht built in 1912 and registered in London. Her original name was Sapphire, but was renamed BREDA by the Royal Navy when she was commandeered. She was 87 meters long and 11 meters wide, weighing in at 1431 GRT (Gross Registered Tonnage). The ship was lost in Campbeltown Lock on 18th February 1944 after being involved in a collision. The official position of the wreck is given as N 55^0 24'.93 W 005^0 34'.95.

At lunch time today we saw a large tall ship approaching the loch, we soon came to realise it was the Tall Ships Youth Trust's (what was once the Sail Training Association) ship "Stavros S Niarchos" and after a lot of manoeuvring she went into the town's harbour alongside the inner quay backwards.

Free Night 32

In her younger years Claire had the privilege of sailing on both the STA's schooners the "Malcolm Miller" and the "Sir Winston Churchill" which were replaced with the two new brigs the "Stavros S Niarchos" and her sister ship "Prince William".

Thursday 7th May 2013, Glenarm Northern Ireland, 19.30 hrs, Sunny and Warm, Baro 1013, Day 246:
Yesterday it blew a hoolie in Campbeltown and we could not believe that the forecast for today could be right, but by 10pm last night the bad weather stopped suddenly. We woke up at 2am to catch the tide and set off across the North Channel for Glenarm in Northern Ireland. The trip ran perfectly according to plan; the weather was fine, the sea moderate and not too sloppy and the tides and course worked fine. We made landfall exactly at noon and spent the remainder of the day soaking up the sunshine and atmosphere of this lovely little marina inside this beautiful old harbour with its white limestone walls and clear emerald green water.

Wednesday 8th May 2013, Glenarm, Rain then Overcast, Baro 986, Day 247:

This morning the rain was torrential and the forecast is for high southerly winds. We are pinned down again by the weather. This afternoon it faired up a little so we took the dogs for a walk on the beach north of the marina where we bumped into the couple from the French boat berthed opposite us. They very kindly invited us to their boat this evening. We went over at 18.30 and stayed until the 20.10 coast guard maritime safety broadcast after which we all retired to the "Bridge" public house for a drink and to use the free Wi-Fi. I was confronted with my first real Irish dilemma. I have heard that to drink Guinness in Ireland is such a good experience that to drink it anywhere else will be a disappointment, and given that I am likely to drink it mostly not in Ireland, this posed quite a risk! . I took my chance and had my first Irish Guinness. Lovely!

Thursday 9th May 2013, Glenarm, 22.00 hrs, SE and Rain, Baro 991, Day 248:

Glenarm is in County Antrim, Northern Ireland and is the ancestral home of the Earls of Antrim. There has been a castle here since the 13th century, and it is at the heart of one of Northern Ireland's oldest estates. Sir Randal MacDonnell, 1st Earl of Antrim built the present castle in 1636. Today the Castle's Walled Garden is open to the public in the summer months and is a venue for a variety of events such as the annual world class Highland Games in July, and the Dalriada Festival which hosts traditional Ulster and Scots cultural events.

According to the town's information boards in 1465 a Franciscan friary was established in Glenarm, there is little left to show for it now and in the mid 1850s Captain Mark Kerr R.N. an experienced seaman had inherited the title and it was his habit to sit in the top of the tower which had been added to the castle in the 1820s. He was something of an eccentric character and was usually attired in a top hat earning him the nick name of "The Conjuror" and hence by association the tower is known as Conjuror's Tower due to his custom of observing the sea through his telescope from the top.

Friday 10th and Sunday 11th May 2013, Larne:
We spent the above two days in Larne loch anchored in shallow water below the Ballylumford power station. An industrial landscape! The weather was less than settled and we endured westerly winds of up to gale force, and sunshine, showers and at times hail stones. We were getting tired as we could not get a good night's sleep due to the necessity to maintain an anchor watch.

Sunday 12th May 2013, Carrickfergus, W5-7 showers, Baro 1008, Day 251:
We left Larne Lough a day earlier than we had intended because more gales were forecast and we did not wish to be stranded in Larne when we needed to be in Carrickfergus.. We arrived in Carrickfergus marina at 14.15hrs on the high tide. Belfast Lough is relatively shallow and according to the pilot books the approach to the marina is prone to silting up, consequently the sea can become somewhat bouncy at the entrance making it hazardous to deep draft vessels. Fortunately Drumlin has a shoal draft and we found our way in without any drama. The staff were very welcoming and helpful.

We spent the evening as guests of our daughter's boyfriend's family and found them to share a similar sense of humour to our own, which is slightly whacky and off the wall. Hannah and Gareth will be arriving on the ferry from Scotland tomorrow.

Monday 13th May 2013, Carrickfergus, W7-8 Showers, Baro 1005, Day 252:
We spent the day exploring Carrickfergus town and took a look around the museum.

Carrickfergus is one of Northern Ireland's most ancient settlements. The walled town 11 miles east of Belfast on the north shore of the Lough, is named after the rock or "carrick" upon which the 6th century King of Dalriada, Fergus was shipwrecked. In 1170 the Anglo-Norman Knight John de Courcy began work building what is now one of Ireland's finest Norman castles on Fergus's Carrick and in 1182 the town's Church dedicated to StNicholas was established. The town has been the scene of many battles and skirmishes throughout its history but significantly in 1599 one Sir Arthur Chichester was instrumental in the importation of mainly protestant Scottish and English settlers, known as planters, who were given land and rights which were denied to the indigenous predominantly Catholic natives. Over the centuries the repercussions caused by the festering wounds so caused has lead to the deep rooted tensions that still exist in Ireland to this day.

In 1637 Carrickfergus relinquished its considerable customs rights, to Belfast causing its importance to decline and the rise in the fortunes of the latter. The 1600s were a turbulent time with the 2 Irish Confederate Wars, both of which resulted in victory for the protestant side, and ultimately in King William of Orange (William III of England and Ireland) landing at the castle in 1690 after it was besieged and fell to the English.

Other points of interest are that the parents of the 7th president of USA, Andrew Jackson (who was to be to the American Indians what the British were to native Irish in 1600s through the Indian Removal Act of 1830) were residents of Carrickfergus prior to their emigration to America in 1765.

The late 1790s witnessed the Irish Rebellion against British rule, and what is now the Carrickfergus Town Hall hosted the controversial trial and execution of William Orr who was a member of the United Irishmen.

The town was known in the 1970s and 80s for its textile and tobacco industries. Today Carrickfergus has Ireland's only surviving coal gasworks, now a museum which began production in 1855 and provided the town with gas for more than a century. Most recently, on his wedding day 29th April 2011, 2nd in line to the British throne, Prince William, was made the first Baron Carrickfergus since 1883.

-oOo-

Hannah and Gareth arrived this evening. The dogs were so pleased to see them, as were we. Hannah was also very excited as Gareth had arranged to take her to Disney World in Florida next week.

Tuesday 14th May 2013, Belfast Abercorn Basin, 21.00 hrs, W5-7 Sunny, Baro 995, Day 253:
A recurring theme we have heard since arriving in Northern Ireland has been "Go into Belfast Abercorn Basin and see the Titanic Museum". This morning, with Hannah and Gareth aboard, we left Carrickfergus bound for Belfast. It seemed in many ways wrong for us in our tiny little yacht to be heading into one of Europe's busiest ports, but everyone assured us it would be alright. It was all very official with big signs on the channel markers instructing approaching vessels to contact

port control by radio. A quick call to Port Control to request permission to proceed was cheerfully granted with a simple instruction to report our arrival in the Basin, which we did. It was quite an experience navigating along the various docks being dwarfed by a bewildering array of vessels both large and colossal being loaded and unloaded by gargantuan mechanical creatures with huge claws and long snouts as they sucked up, spat out and mauled the very innards of these maritime leviathans. We felt quite insignificant, like an ant in a farmyard.

We arrived safely in the basin and our surroundings were as beautiful as the weather, bathed as we were in warm sunshine and encompassed by the classy new waterfront development which is the Titanic Quarter.

In the afternoon Gareth left us to "go shopping for something", and Claire, Hannah and I visited the Titanic Museum. This is quite a remarkable visitor attraction, not only celebrating the Harland and Wolff Shipyard's achievement of constructing what was at the time the world's largest movable manmade object, RMS Titanic, but also the social history of Belfast and Ireland as a whole in the Edwardian and pre First World War era.

Wednesday 15th May 2013, Carrickfergus, NW5-7, Baro 996, Day 254:
We returned to Carrickfergus from Belfast's Abercorn Basin this morning. The port was very busy and we passed a huge white American Cruise liner called "Artania" on her way in. Just to put this in some sort of perspective Titanic was 269 meters long and weighed in at 52,310 tons, Artania is 230m long and 44,348 tons. If my calculations are correct Titanic was nearly a quarter as big again as this awe-inspiring floating playground! Boy did we feel small!

The lough was very windy and quite rough and we had to stay well clear of the ferries coming and going in the main channel.

In the evening we met up with Hannah, Gareth and his family for a meal at a local restaurant to celebrate his 21st birthday. Afterwards we adjourned to their family home to continue the festivities. That's when it happened. Gareth managed to take me on one side and revealed the purpose of his clandestine shopping trip in Belfast yesterday. He wanted my blessing to ask Hannah to marry him whilst away at Disney World next week; a blessing I was more than happy to give. Gareth is a fine young man who is clearly besotted with Hannah.

Friday 17th May 2013, Larne, 22.00 hrs, NW 4-5 Sunny, Baro 1012, Day 256:
We left Carrickfergus on our first leg north back to Scotland today. The weather is looking promising for Sunday so the plan is to remain here tomorrow. I rang the East Antrim Yacht Club when we arrived and they kindly said we could use a mooring, so this time we are not anchoring, they also kindly sent someone over in a RIB to escort us to a suitable mooring for our size of boat. Once settled in Claire began cooking tea and just before it was ready a young man probably in his mid teens came over in a motor boat inviting us to go ashore to the Yacht Club as on a Friday night they put on a meal. Sadly we had to decline. Once again we were impressed by the friendliness and hospitality of the Irish.

Hannah rang to say she and Gareth had arrived safely at Heathrow ready for their flight tomorrow to Disney World Florida. She was very excited.

Free night 35

109

Saturday 18th May 2013, Larne, 12.00 hrs, NW3 Rain, Day 257:

Hannah and Gareth are safely on their way to America and we are watching the weather. As things stand we may decide to set off to Glenarm tonight in order to get the best start tomorrow for Islay.

Glenarm, Still Raining, Baro 1009:

We motored up from Larne to Glenarm this evening. We intend to set off across the North Channel early tomorrow for Islay. Let us hope my planning and the weather forecast is good as this is a long passage and the weather for the rest of the week looks quite ferocious.

It is worthy of note to include here the fact that Claire rang Billy the Harbour Master at Glenarm to tell him of our intension to arrive later this evening and depart early tomorrow morning. The toilet facilities at Glenarm are outside the marina gate and they both require an electronic key to gain access, and the marina office closes at tea time. Billy, however, took the trouble to wait for us knowing we would otherwise not be able to use the shore side facilities. That is a kindness and courtesy above and beyond the call of duty and we were very grateful to him for taking so much trouble.

Chapter Six

Back in Scotland

"The power men possess to annoy me, I
give them by a weak curiosity. No
man can come near me but
through my act." [19]
Ralph Waldo Emerson

Sunday 19th May 2013, Islay, 21.12 hrs, Fog and Calm, Baro 1017, Day 258:
We departed Glenarm at about 7am in thick fog. Fortunately we have radar, a chart plotter and a GPS, so we had extra eyes. Had we not had the radar we would not have contemplated setting off as the risk level would have been unacceptably high. As it turned out creeping along slowly and "flying on instruments" we made a safe exit into clear water.

The heavy rain on Saturday had caused flash floods during the night and a staggering amount of debris was washed down the rivers of Northern Ireland into the sea including logs and pieces of trees. Initially we thought a cargo ship had shed its load of timber and we took turns at the bows as spotter to avoid hitting the treacherous semi submerged log battering rams hiding camouflaged against the dross of bark and leaves floating on the surface.

By the time we were in the middle of the North Channel heading nearly due north for the Mull of Kintyre, the fog was thinning out and lifting.

There is a Traffic Separation Scheme at the entrance to the North Channel to assist large ships to navigate the relatively narrow shipping lane safely, and we, as a small leisure vessel, would be persona non grata within it. Bicycles are not allowed on motorways, it's the same idea, so we had to travel to the east of it to avoid it before turning North West for Islay. This added a few extra miles to the voyage not to mention a number of extra hours.

We arrived in Port Ellen at about 6pm and moored up on a visitor mooring buoy. It is beautiful here. Hannah and Gareth emailed to say they had safely arrived in Florida which in turn alerted us to the fact that the 3G mobile telephone signal was much stronger and more reliable here than on the mainland in Troon!

Free Night 36

Tuesday 21st May 2013, Port Ellen Islay, NW3-4, Baro 1022, Day 260:
We received a message from Hannah in Florida last night saying she was worried about a tornado that had been reported on the television news. They were experiencing a bad tropical storm. The tornado hit Oklahoma City and was reported to be 2 miles wide and had killed 91 people. Today the authorities revised that number down to 24, still devastating for those involved! Fortunately it was not near to where Hannah and Gareth were.

I inflated the dinghy today intending to take advantage of the reasonably calm water and lighter wind to walk the dogs, but when I launched it I heard a hissing noise. It was punctured, possibly done on the stanchion when I tipped it over the side. I repaired it, but the glue is supposed to be allowed to cure for 24 hours so I shall wait until tomorrow and try again.

Free Night 38

Wednesday 22nd May 2013, Port Ellen, Wind 5-7, Baro 1024, Day 261:

We re-launched the dinghy which seems to be holding its air in now. It nearly blew over as we did so, but she is now safely lashed to the stern of Drumlin like a baby elephant to the tail of its mother. It is far too windy for it to be safe to attempt to go ashore.

I briefly saw a bird fly over our stern and return to the shore which appeared to be some sort of bird of prey. After discussions with Claire, who is usually very reliable concerning matters of avian identification and recognition, we decided it was probably a peregrine falcon.

We later saw a similar bird at much closer quarters near Gigha on our return passage in August which positively identified the mystery bird. It was in fact an arctic skua.

I also composed and sent a potted history of our travels so far to friends and family by email after I fixed the water pump which had worked its way loose from its mounting under the sink this morning. It has been a quiet day confined to barracks due to the windy weather. Gareth proposed to Hannah today in the Little Mermaid's Grotto in Disney World!

Free Night 39

From:"drumlin@sea.co.uk"
To:
Subject: The Dalby Adventures

Date: Wed, May 22, 2013 15:53

Well it's been on my mind for a while to contact various people, but getting round to it is the thing. Most of the time we don't have laptop internet, just the phone and that can be unreliable depending on where we are. At the moment we are in Port Ellen on Islay.

Last summer we basically sold up, bought Drumlin our yacht in Glasson near Lancaster and sailed to Troon in Scotland via Ramsey on the Isle of Man.

After a settled period over winter in Troon we set out on our nomadic adventures on 2nd April. First we went up Loch Fyne via Port Bannatyne on Bute after negotiating the narrows at the Kyles of Bute. We saw an otter on one of the islands there. A brief return to Troon saw us meet up with my Dad then we headed back to Rothesay for a week then across to Innellen Bay on the Clyde. It was like parking in a lay-by on the A1, a constant stream of traffic, much of the big stuff Royal Navy. We stayed one night! We then relocated to Millport on the Isle of Great Cumbrae for a few days. The chip shop on the front is excellent, run by a Turkish chap who spent 10 years at the Wetherby Whaler in York, so he has a good pedigree. Only thing, no mushy peas. Personally I can't stand them but Claire is keen. We were really killing a bit of time because Hannah wanted to meet up with us in Northern Ireland on 15th May with her boyfriend Gareth to celebrate his 21st birthday. So we headed to Campbeltown on the Mull of Kintyre after a 5 day sojourn in Lamlash bay on the Isle of Arran to await favourable conditions to head across the notorious North Channel to Ireland.

Eventually the opportunity presented itself and we struck out on the 34 mile open sea passage to the only country of the United Kingdom we have never visited. 10 hours later, having weighed anchor at 2am for the tide, we drew alongside the visitor pontoon in the delightful village of Glenarm in glorious sunshine. We stayed 3 days and befriended a French couple who were working their way home to Roscof having been as far north as Svalbard in Norway!

As the big day of Gareth's 21st approached we moved south stopping in Larne Lough then finally round into Belfast Lough and Carrickfergus. What a lovely place. A beautiful Norman castle, loads of history and forget anything you've been told about friendly Irish hospitality, it doesn't even come close. EVERYONE was so nice and friendly and helpful I cannot begin to describe it. And top of the agenda is how to save the most money and get the best of what is on offer. We arrived on the Monday, met Hannah and Gareth and visited his family home in the evening. On Tuesday Hannah and Gareth came aboard Drumlin and we sailed right into Abercorn Basin in the centre of Belfast. Cheapest marina I have ever been in and not the worst by a country mile. That afternoon we went round ... You guessed it, the Titanic experience. It is actually as much about the social history of early 20th century Belfast as it is specifically about the ships, and again as someone interested in history, it was worth seeing. Mind you at £14.75 per person you shed tears on the way in as well as at the exit! The next day, Wednesday, we ran the gauntlet of the harbour and returned to Carrickfergus for the big bash. A good time was had by all.

On the Thursday Hannah and Gareth left for home in Thirsk and then for Florida where they are spending their second week of holiday at Disney World.

We slowly made our way back to Glenarm in preparation for the 40 mile passage to the island of Islay. We left at 6am on Sunday 19th in a pea soup fog. Thank heavens for GPS, chart plotters and radar. The murk soon lifted as we cleared the coast and we had an uneventful crossing to Port Ellen.

As I sit here rambling we are on a mooring in the bay waiting for another gale to pass through. Yes, yet another. We cannot remember when we last went over a week without the Coast Guard issuing a gale warning. But it is sunny.

So where next? Roughly we think Gigha, Ardfern then Oban. Watch this space.

We hope this email finds you all well and that life is treating you at least as kindly as it is us.

Andy and Claire.

-oOo-

Thursday 23rd May 2013, Port Ellen, NW 8-9 Sunny, Baro 1021, Day 262:
It has been VERY windy, so much so that a Royal Navy minesweeper came into the bay to anchor and the Calmac Ferry had difficulty berthing in the harbour! Naturally we didn't go ashore. The news today has been full of the Woolwich Murder that took place yesterday. We reap what we sow, but when the state sows it's the poor individual that pays the price every time.

Lee Rigby was a private soldier in the Royal Regiment of Fusiliers of the British Army, who was murdered whilst off duty on a street in Woolwich, London by two British men of Nigerian descent, Michael Olumide Adebolajo and Michael Oluwatobi Adebowale. They claimed to be Christian converts to Islam acting to avenge the Killing of Muslims by British forces abroad. Their trial began at the Old Bailey on 29 November 2013 and on 19 December 2013 they were found guilty of Rigby's murder. They will be sentenced by Judge Mr Justice Sweeney after he has the verdict of the appeal court's ruling on the use of whole life terms.

-oOo-

Friday 24th May 2013, Port Ellen, NW3 Sunny, Baro 1022, Day 263:
Finally we made it ashore and it was well worth the wait. Port Ellen is a great place with lovely beaches and the dogs enjoyed their first taste of freedom in 6 days. Today the weather has been sunny and reasonably warm.

Islay was once the capital of the western isles, originally part of the kingdom of Dalriada from about the 6th century with strong links to Ireland. A notable Irish link is St Columba who called at Islay on his way to Iona in the 6th Century. The island was taken into Norse rule and was a Viking stronghold from the 9th century becoming part of the Kingdom of the Isles. Somerled King of Argyll was a notable leader of this period founding the clan M^{ac}Donald and re-uniting what had become a divided Kingdom in 1164. This regime continued until the Treaty of Perth in 1266 when the Hebrides became part of the Kingdom of Scotland. In 1493 the M^{ac}Donalds were unable to meet their obligations to support their King, James IV of Scotland, and their lands and titles were forfeit.

In Victorian times Islay was, like much of the Scotland, subject to ethnic cleansing which is euphemistically referred to in history books as "the clearances" which considered it an improvement to the land to forcibly evict and deport people in favour of sheep because sheep farming was more profitable than having tenants, and by implication money and profit are more important than people!

> "Maybe it is a general truth that those
> who do most damage to the
> world are those who try
> to improve it." [20]
> Ian Mitchell

Today Islay is a whisky producer par exellence!

Free Night 41

Saturday 25th May 2013, Ardminish Bay Gigha, S2-3 Sunny, Baro 1022, Day 264:

We set sail from Port Ellen this morning after calling in to the pontoons to take on water. Whilst we were there we saw a replica of St Columba's wooden framed skin covered boat called a currach measuring some 30 feet in length, similar to Drumlin, which the saint had used in AD563 to sail to Iona bringing Christianity to Scotland. This replica was on its way back home to Northern Ireland's second largest city, The united Kingdom's 2013 City of Culture, Derry (Londonderry) having visited Iona Abbey as part of the 75th anniversary of the setting up of the Iona Community by the Reverend George M[ac]Leod in 1938. Incidentally Saint Columba is the Patron Saint of Derry.

Gigha was visited by our old friend King Haakon on his way to Largs in 1263 and again on his way back. In the 1530s – 1550s the Island, which belonged to the M[ac]Neills, was plundered and harassed by various pirates and feuding clan warlords, but in 1554 it was restored to them. The island was lately owned by Sir James Horlick who's name is now associated with a malted milk beverage of the same name, but it has now been in the possession of the island's residents since 2002 in the form of the Gigha Heritage Trust.

Gigha is a thoroughly lovely island, but I have to admit that the more time I spent there the more irritated I became with it. It is the only place to stop along the west coast of the Mull of Kintyre and is the one place a passing yachtsman would want to be able to take on water and buy in provisions. The fact is you cannot, when we were there, there was no shop and no shore access except by dinghy. What is more it seems that the local residents have to go to the mainland for practically every one of life's necessities. It was probably from this point onwards that I really began to get into my stride with the protest poetry! I also wrote the following commentary on my mobile telephone's note pad on 28th May because when at sea we cannot use the laptop. It is not in italics as it was not a diary entry.

Tuesday 28th May 2013, Gigha, Day 267:
Now call me a curmudgeonly old grump, but I had a bit of a moan this morning about Gigha. Let me put it into some sort of context. Gigha is a west coast island owned by its inhabitants, well a residents' cooperative of some sort. In 2001, according to Wikipedia, the population was 110 and in 2002 they bought the island. It has an hourly CalMac ferry service, and anyone wanting to live here must make an application to the cooperative and also have a skill or trade required by the island. Now at this point I am on the verge of spontaneous combustion because, as laudable as this policy sounds, I believe it to be complete hogwash. Let me explain.

On the face of it bringing skills and trades to the island sounds like it will boost the economy, right? Wrong! An economy should not be mendicant. If people want to come to these island places one imagines they are in search of that authentic island life, either as a resident or indeed a tourist.

What is authentic island life? I assume it is a way of life primarily, if not able to be completely nowadays, self-reliant and largely independent and set apart from the mainstream rat race of mainland life.

What have I found on Gigha? A theme park! An overpriced, money grabbing tourist trap populated by people behaving like tribal natives caricaturing themselves to exploit the contents of the pockets of unthinking, undiscerning holidaymakers! Now at this point I imagine you are revving up to some defensive position of indignation on behalf of the poor downtrodden islanders struggling to make a living in an ever increasingly globalised world. Let me finish.

As far as I can see there is nothing sustainable happening on the island beyond a bit of small scale farming and a few wind generators. It has no economy. A hotel, a rip off cafe come restaurant and a post office open for two hours a day; hardly the makings of a thriving self-reliant economy. Everything they need they must bring over, on the ferry. There seems to be little work. What they are doing is using what they earn to feather their nest by upgrading the housing stock and creating an exclusive enclave for rich hippies and retired stockbrokers. Take away the ferry, and the island will become a rock star's retreat with a population of five in no time at all as the population collapses under its own weight. It is unsustainable and does not deserve to survive. They are missing the opportunity to build an economy. The place needs shops, a butcher, a baker, a green grocer. Where are the traditional crafts the weavers and knitters? Please, no more tartan wool shops selling tins of shortbread, silly tartan hats and twee CDs of Scottish folk songs sung by Flora M^{ac}Whocares we never heard of her anyway. And what is the big planned improvement they are aiming for? Better pontoons to get rich yachties ashore to spend in their overpriced, just what Gigha needs, one or two individuals with their "make a packet by exploiting visitors businesses," and stuff the island's future.

Hello people of Gigha, you've been rumbled. Stop pretending this is about reviving island life and call it what it is, "A great scam designed to maximise your investment." If it was about the island; ferry or no ferry, visitors or none, you'd be happy, willing and most importantly able to carry on fending for yourselves, each of you providing essential goods and services for those next to you. That is an economy! That is authentic island life! Independence from the outside, and co-dependence by those on the island. Sure, the place was buzzing, especially on a bank holiday weekend or when the cruise liner anchors offshore and brings in the passengers for half an hour to "do" Gigha, but honestly, when the six or eight children in the school grow up, what will they do? Gigha: God's island; and you have reduced it to an amusement park...

Since writing the above criticism I have not been able to satisfy myself enough to charge the ferry service to Gigha with being subsidised by the tax payer. I know that the Road Equivalent Tariff or RET is applied to some ferry services effectively reducing the ferry fares to a price that they consider equal to that which one would pay for the same journey by road. According to the Calmac website the company is entirely owned by the Scottish government.

In simple terms the ferry is provided and owned by the tax payer and it is right that government should provide isolated communities with modern communications of all kinds, but often good intensions have unintended consequences. Islands should not be enabled or even allowed to degenerate into moated housing estates for rich commuters, holiday parks for those who can afford second homes or gated communities for the wealthy retired. In my view authentic island life should be about communities and people going about their daily business **ON** the island otherwise it isn't authentic island life. I suppose the same argument and criticisms can be made of many villages and of village life. It is just that out here the corrosive effects of modern day life on communities and local economies are so much more obvious.

-oOo-

Wednesday 29th May 2013, Ardminish Bay, NW4-5 Very Sunny, Baro 1020, Day 268:

We spent most of the day sitting in the cockpit enjoying the sunshine and sheltering from the breeze. I did have a small mishap, when I stood up and my head rose above the shelter of the spray hood, the wind took hold of my cap and blew it into the sea. It headed off downwind quite quickly and looked as if it would either be lost or sunk in no time at all. I gave up hope and went below for a cup of tea. We could still see it after I had finished drinking my conciliatory cuppa so I decided to take to the dinghy and retrieve it. This would have made quite a good comedy video for one of those television shows that makes entertainment out of the mishaps and misfortune of the incompetent and unfortunate! Because the wind was sufficiently strong, each time I came alongside "the casualty" and had stopped the engine, it had blown me several meters downwind putting it quite out of reach! I had come this far I was not going to be beaten, and indeed after numerous attempts, much to the amusement of the other yacht crews and bystanders on the shore, I finally recovered my cap and triumphantly returned to a hero's welcome aboard

Drumlin. This is the great achievement of my 51st birthday, for today is my birthday, and my first as a nomad of the sea and to celebrate we went to the "Boathouse", a charming little theme restaurant on the beach. Claire's haddock and chips were the best she'd had for a long time, in fact the only fish and chips she'd had since our rendezvous with the Turkish fish fryer from York in Millport. My 8oz burger and chips were in fact two 4oz burgers, but nevertheless a welcome digression from our usual predominantly vegetarian fare.

Free Night 45

Welcome to the land of missed opportunity

Welcome to the land of missed opportunity,
A land of want, but what you want.
Welcome to the land of rich exclusivity,
Where ghosts of reality haunt.

Here is a place that offers us all,
A place grown ripe to enjoy,
Here is a place with a siren call,
But a place of no true employ.

Once a community, vibrant, alive,
Each playing their part in the whole,
Now an illusion, a mendicant tribe,
It's now just a mem'ry, a shadow, no soul.

Where is the butcher, the baker, the tink?
And what of the weaver, the tanner or smith?
Where are jobs which sever the link,
And, what independence? A myth!

So let's go to Gigha to live the dream,
Return to well being and jolly good health,
And proving ones worth as one of the team,
A return on investment and wealth.

Quite unsustainable! Invalid their goal,
Relies on the ferry to supply what they need,
Quite what the future will hold can't be told,
Defies any logic this illusory creed.

This island life that we all want to treasure,
This corner of heaven on earth,
Doesn't deserve in any small measure,
To survive whilst under this curse.

So people of Gigha and those of your ilk,
Get wise to the folly you sow,
Your island's not flowing with honey or milk,
It needs planting and tending and help to grow.

It is your duty you must realise,
Your task so hard to perform,
But per ardua ad astra, reach for the skies,
And true island life be reborn.

Andrew Dalby, Ardfern 7th June 2013

Thursday 30th May 2013, Fairy Isles Loch Sween, N4-5
Sunny, Baro 1020, Day 269:
We left Gigha in blazing sunshine and a forecast NW wind.
Actually the wind was Northerly all the way! In days of old
people believed the words of prophets and seers, today we
have the Met Office; purveyors and pedlars of pseudo-
scientific necromancy that anyone with a flag and a piece of
seaweed could accomplish. They are so vague and imprecise I

sometimes think it is hardly worth the effort tuning in. Here is a typical example:
"Visibility good to moderate, occasionally poor."

Translates into:
"You might be able to see, then again, maybe not"!

And before the Met Office brings a lawsuit against me for libel, I am joking! It is real science and a necessary part of a sailor's life, but please; instead of hedging your bets, if you don't know just say so!

Having swapped Gigha, the island with no shop, for Tayvallich, we find ourselves perched on the edge of a rather small anchorage already populated by 3 other yachts because the whole of Tayvallich Bay, both inside and out, is stuffed with moorings leaving nowhere to anchor. Furthermore there is a fee to pay for the visitor moorings, £10. They take away the free parking and put in parking you must pay for! Oh no, not me. It is a rip off. The pilot book is also woefully out of date as it says there is anchoring room in the bay, and considering I bought it new this year for £25 I could have enjoyed 2 and a half nights moored.

So, having motored into wind in search of a place to anchor near a shop where I can finally obtain provisions, "there is no room in the inn." 2 thousand years and the story never changes, we have to sleep outside with the animals. Just to put this into context for everyone who is thinking to themselves, "It's only a tenner," may I remind you that £10 is a third, yes 33% of our weekly disposable income. Would you pay the equivalent of that out of your money to park to get your shopping, even in a rural place like this? No, I thought not.
Free Night 46

Once again I wrote the following commentary on my mobile telephone's note pad on 31st and it too is not in italics as it was not a diary entry.

Well today is Friday 31st May 2013. Yesterday we arrived in Tayvallich where the pilot book assures an anchorage and village with facilities. We'd arrived at about 8 in the evening to a bay congested to the point of overrun with private moorings, quite a number unused, and fee to pay visitor moorings. Needless to say I had another rage induced by the money grabbing commercialism of it all. We decided to try the outer bay only to find it completely occupied by a commercial dive boat and floating pontoons used as lobster pot storage. We went round to the Fairy Isles to anchor for the night. This morning, calmer, I resolved to go back in and anchor with a tripping line and jolly well go ashore for essential supplies and bloody well not pay the £10 mooring fee! However, when we were in the bay we decided to try the pontoon for ease of access and discovered stays of 2 hours or less are free. That, and a refreshingly well stocked shop that didn't break the bank, restored my faith to some degree. We filled up with water too and were pleased to discover we've only used half a tank in a week. Whilst there we were rafted up against by the 44ft "Damsis" a charter yacht which we had shared the anchorage with last night. The crew, Mum, Dad two grandparents and the triplets are lovely people and between us we emptied the shop!!!

We returned to the anchorage shortly afterwards joined by Damsis and another yacht called Curlew. Her crew was a bloke and two teenage boys. Once their dinghies were out and the kids aboard the afternoon's entertainment began. So marks out of ten for Tayvallich, 5. If Gigha only merits nil, Tayvallich gets a middle score because one can resupply conveniently without being ripped off. I'm happy for myself, but Tayvallich would probably have done better out of us if we could stay longer to enjoy it. Like our old home town of Thirsk, the parking issue is not a boost to tourism! It seems to me that once again a business, in this case Tayvallich Bay Authority, is profiting at the village's expense. People of Tayvallich, you are being exploited, wake up and benefit yourselves. Reclaim your bay, revive your community and grow an economy. As for the shop, it was staffed by a man who had tried this liveaboard life and lasted three months because of the continual bad weather and high winds in the Hebrides, but he ran a good shop suiting and meeting the needs of his community and visiting yachtsmen. Well done him.

> "I cannot consent to pay for
> a privilege where I have
> intrinsic right." [21]
> Ralph Waldo Emerson

Statists or capitalists might deny that anyone has intrinsic rights to freedom of movement or indeed the right to stop still! I would suggest that such a view is the result of social conditioning to accept as normal the unacceptable power the few exercise over the many and the oppression of the individual.

-oOo-

Friday 31st May 2013, Fairy Isles Loch Sween, Wind 2-3 Part Cloud, Baro 1024, Day 270:
We awoke to the very quiet and beautiful surroundings of the Fairy Isles, a tiny lagoon just north of the village of Tayvallich. The ancient woodlands and volcanic rock gives this place an atmosphere not unlike the English Lake District and it is very calm and sheltered.

After eating breakfast we went round into the village with the intention of anchoring on a very short chain in the safest spot we could find with one of us going ashore to do some shopping, however once in the village bay we discovered that the pontoon hammer head is designated as a short stay berth for yachts using the village facilities and has a water supply too. Although I am not entirely happy that the village has effectively made anchoring practically impossible within the bay, this small olive branch has in some way soothed my indignation from yesterday evening. We had not been moored many minutes when "Damsis", a Bavaria 44, and one of the yachts sharing the anchorage with us last night came alongside and rafted up to us on the outside; being half as long again as Drumlin we felt rather dwarfed.

We returned to the anchorage for a second night after an excellent shopping expedition. The afternoon was beautifully sunny and we spent most of it reading and watching the children from Damsis exploring the creeks in their inflatable boats and finding mussels in great abundance which they kindly shared with us. Claire cooked them (the mussels not the children) in a sauce of butter, onions, parsley and cheese - They were delicious!

Free Meal 1 – Free Night 47

Saturday 1st June 2013, Fairy Isles, SW2-3 Cloudy then Sunny, Baro 1026, Day 271:
We spent a chilly morning reading in the saloon. Two of the three other yachts anchored over night left leaving us alone with a very large 55 feet long Hallberg-Rassy yacht. The sun came out this afternoon and our last remaining neighbour set off for Ardfern after enquiring if we had seen the ospreys. We hadn't. They left. We saw! Almost as soon as they were out of sight a commotion in the sky above us announced their majestic presence. Meanwhile on the small island opposite we

noticed a mute swan serenely sitting on her nest where she remained alone for the rest of the day.

There has been a steady stream of sea kayaks stealthily paddling past today too. Like most wildlife if you sit quietly long enough you are often rewarded with a sighting, unlike most wildlife they do have a habit of catching you unaware. An unexpected and hearty, "Hail fellow well met" from the blind side of a dodger is a guaranteed method of spilling a precious dram of fine single malt!

There is no VHF or mobile phone signal here so short of breeding carrier pigeons, launching a message in a bottle or lighting a fire for smoke signals we are alone.

Free Night 48

Sunday 2nd June, Craignish Lagoon Ardfern, SW2-3 Sun/Haze, Baro 1033, Day 272:
We left the Fairy Isles at 7am and motored down Loch Sween and negotiated our way out past the islands and tidal race at the entrance to the loch. It was very calm and sunny, but chilly! The day gradually warmed up and when we were just south of Crinan we managed to hoist both sails and goose-winged into Loch Craignish. We had planned to drop the hook in the anchorage by Eilean Inshaig outside Ardfern but, surprise surprise, the entire area was infested with the marina's moorings making anchoring virtually impossible. We relocated to the lagoon a mile further south.

Free night 49

Monday 3rd June 2013, Craignish Lagoon Ardfern, 21.00 hrs, SW2 Sunny, Baro 1034, Day 273:
It has been another beautiful warm and sunny day. We went ashore and walked the mile or so to the village shop and marina this morning. Happily we bumped into the gentleman from the

Fairy Isles who had enquired about the ospreys. He was genuinely pleased to know that they were still thriving. On the way back to the boat we noticed that the mast head light was at a jaunty angle perched rather like the top hat of a Victorian down and out, so when back aboard I climbed the mast to investigate. I was dismayed to find that the lens cover had previously been broken and repaired with tape which had perished. This will have to be replaced with a new one when we are back in Troon. Fortunately we have alternative lights to use if we sail at night, it is just that the mast head lights use the least amount of power and are high up and can been seen more easily.

We saw two wild goats on Eilean Mhic Chrion which is the island opposite forming the northern half of the east side of the lagoon. Apparently there is a herd of wild goats reputedly living there.

Free Night 50

Tuesday 4th June 2013, Craignish Lagoon, W2 or Variable Sunny, Baro 1028, Day 274:
It has been another lovely sunny day much warmer outside than in. This morning I rowed the dinghy across to the islands that run along the eastern edge of the lagoon to explore and Claire remained aboard making a dodger for the transom and doing a little laundry. Whilst I was on the island Eilean Dubh I saw a hen shelduck and the ribs and keel of a wrecked boat on the beach. A little further inland and up the shore I came across two stone structures. They were hard to interpret from the vantage point I had, and seemed to me to be too small for animal enclosures and they had no obvious suggestions of human occupation such as the remnants of a hearth, doors or windows. As to their vintage it was impossible to tell if they were recent or prehistoric. There are several ancient buildings noted on the charts on the surrounding islands and duns were apparently built to protect the head of the loch in Iron Age times. There is an island on the

130

east side of the loch partly visible from here called Eilean Righ which means the king's island suggesting that this was probably an important area in antiquity and possibly linked to the Scandinavian King Olav.

During the afternoon I decided that it might be a good idea to go for a swim off the ladder at the back of the boat. I was wrong; it was a bad idea for although the air was warm the water certainly was not. In order to restore circulation and the feeling in my extremities I took the dogs ashore for a walk instead.

Free Night 51

Craignish

Spend a day in Craignish lagoon,
With lots of sunshine, a breeze a boon,
The peace and quiet save songs of birds,
Where nature speaks her silent words,
The warming rays of sun's pure light,
Pray lux eterna, delay the night!
To dream away the time of day,
Where fishes leap and otters play,
A day spent thus in calm repose,
To take a swim without your clothes,
And feel that sense of God close by,
Craignish Lagoon where ospreys fly!

Andrew Dalby, Ardfern, 4th June 2013

Wednesday 5th June 2013, Craignish Lagoon Ardfern, Variable2 and Sunny, Baro 1022, Day 275:
We passed the day in similar fashion to yesterday strenuously engaging in leisure. I paddled over to Eilean Mhic Chrion where

the goats are, only to find it looked more inviting than it really was. The ground is hard to walk over being vegetation covered boulders, and its hillside rises more steeply than the interest on a payday loan. Instead I made my way over to Eilean Dubh to explore the east side. I found a secret stash of lobster pots and sundry fishing items buried in the cleft of a rock and a number of items of clothing suspended in a tree!

This evening's entertainment came in the form of the Craignish lagoon canoe club's children who spent a couple of hours skating around the lagoon in multi coloured kayaks, but the highlight of the day was a man walking on water. Actually it transpired that the gentleman was standing on a surf board and he silently and deftly propelled himself along with a canoe paddle. The water was as calm and smooth as a mirror and he disappeared to the south. We did not witness his return.

Free Night 52

On our daily walks ashore with the dogs Claire and I met the same retired local lady a number of times. She told us that she has resided in the village since she was 14 months old and good manners prevents me from disclosing how many years ago that was. Suffice it to say, this sprightly and charming lady can recall the days when the, "Marina was no more than a hut on stilts" long before the tourists arrived. Her local knowledge is considerable and I recall one sunny afternoon leaning against a gate with her overlooking the Lagoon whilst she spoke about life in this remote and beautiful part of Scotland. She liked to see visiting yachts anchored and expressed resentment at the arrival of pay-to-stay mooring buoys in the lagoon as a cynical attempt to make money. She is not a boater and had no obvious axe to grind. She just seemed to say it was not wanted.

Another trip ashore resulted in another chance encounter with a local gentleman. He was in the process of climbing into his dinghy to row out to his boat moored on a private mooring. We exchanged pleasantries which included my volunteering the fact that I was anchored in the lagoon. With no further prompting he made a point of telling me how welcome yachts are to come here and anchor!

I must make it clear that the marina in Ardfern are not responsible for the Lagoon pay-to-stay mooring buoys.

Thursday 6th June 2013, Craignish Lagoon Ardfern, W2
Sunny, Baro 1023, Day 276:
It has been another lovely day and I circumnavigated Eilean Buidhe at the southern end of the lagoon. I managed to ghost along reasonably quietly and approached a family of seals sunbathing on some rocks, but they knew I was there and swam away before I drifted too close. We have seen the goats on Eilean Mhic Chrion again along with a deer. This afternoon whilst I was exploring the island there was a VERY loud bang from Eilean Righ. When I returned to Drumlin, Claire said that she had seen a small Royal Navy boat go ashore and blow something up on the beach!

I have since learned from an ex Royal Navy sailor that there is a large amount of unexploded ordinance in these parts, a legacy of the Second World War, that periodically floats to the surface or washes ashore. He told me that there is always a Navy vessel on duty to deal with these things and that was probably what had happened.
Bracken fell out of the dinghy in his eagerness to get to shore for his walk. The score for dunkings now stands at Bracken 3: Chip 2!

Just to the south of us there are a number of yachts moored, one is blue and has beautiful classic lines. We have noticed that a local man comes to her most evenings and sails her off her mooring, often singlehanded, noiselessly sweeping round the lagoon, and she performs a perfect graceful arabesque as she returns to her mooring under sail. And not a drop of fuel burned! A master class in sailing.

Free Night 53

Saturday 8th June 2013, Eilean Nan Gabhar (Goat Island) Craignish, 21.40 hrs, Variable or SW1-2 Sunny, Baro 1022, Day 278:
We abruptly ran out of water last night so we had to call upon the jerry can emergency supply in the locker. This prompted us to weigh anchor this morning and go into Ardfern Marina for fuel and water. That achieved we motored southwards down the east side of Eilean Righ to this anchorage and spent the rest of the day in solitude and glorious sunshine. I visited all the islands around us save the tiny one with the nesting birds. Tomorrow we intend to head off through the Dorus Mor with the tide and head up the sound of Luing to Kerrera, the island opposite Oban.

Free Night 55

Eilean Rìgh is an interesting piece of real estate. Its name means King's Island, but which king is the subject of some conjecture. Historically it has been a place of some importance as it has two Iron Age forts. It is interesting to know that it belonged to one Sir Reginald Johnson who is famed for having been the tutor of Puyi, China's last Emperor. Indeed Johnson's oriental influence can be seen in the distinctly Buddhist style of the buildings he modernised. At the time of writing this island is for sale for offers over £3,000,000.00. I wish I'd known!!!

Chapter Seven

Pastures New

"Hic sunt dracones – Here are dragons."
Hunt-Lenox Globe, circa 1510

If you discount the first part of our adventure sailing from Glasson to Troon because we were starting in a new place and travelling to a familiar one, Troon, and overlook the fact that when we left there at the start of this season we went to Northern Ireland, a place we had never visited before, the next part of our adventure begins here. In our early days of sailing as holiday boaters we had been to Campbeltown and around the Mull of Kintyre to Islay on a sailing school yacht and indeed even to Ardfern albeit via the Crinan Canal aboard Rachel, our dear little Seawych. Now, however, we were about to embark upon a real test because we were heading into an unfamiliar area through some very challenging tidal waters strewn with hazards and perils.

Sunday 9th June 2013, Little Horseshoe Bay Kerrera, S2 Sunny, Baro 1013, Day 279:
We made our passage through Dorus Mor and the sound of Luing just as planned and without incident except that Claire saw two Seals actually fighting in the water. It was probably a territorial dispute. Because of the combination of the seabed, which is as rugged as the mountains on the land around us, coupled with a formidably strong tidal stream the surface of the sea in this area has eddies and whirlpools that would not seem out of place on an alpine river in spate and the scene changed from very interesting to plain spectacular as we motored at over 10 knots past the Fladda Light House at the

northern end of the sound where the passage is at its narrowest. Mercifully we were doing this in perfect conditions. (Drumlin usually potters along at a steady 4 or 5 knots under power, the extra speed was simply due to the fact that the sea was flowing along underneath us in the same direction as we were and going at about 5 or six knots. Just like walking along a moving escalator!) *It was gratifying to manage to sail some of the way once we had cleared the tidal race and entered the Firth of Lorn preserving some of our fuel.*

On anchoring in Little Horseshoe Bay, which is towards the south end of Kerrera Sound, I heard a familiar noise, that of parrots squawking. I am very fond of psittacines and until quite recently I kept an aviary. Thanks to the wonders of the internet I learned that this was the Island Parrot Sanctuary, a rescue centre doing valuable work for beautiful birds that for whatever reason are in need of care and a good home.

Free Night 56

Tuesday 11th June 2013, Horseshoe Bay Kerrera, S2-4 Rain, Baro 1009, Day 280:
We decided to relocate to Horseshoe Bay, the larger bay just a short distance north of Little Horseshoe Bay because we were unhappy about the available depth of water and an underwater cable that we could have potentially snagged. Unlike yesterday it has been too wet to paint, but I did manage a little varnishing around the companionway.

History records that this bay is where Alexander II of Scotland died when he anchored his fleet in 1249. Apparently he was on his way to "help" Ewen Lord of Argyll to decide to sever his allegiance to Haakon IV of Norway because he had rejected his earlier polite suggestion that he should! Also can you guess who else anchored here? Yes, our old friend

Haakon anchored here both on his way to and on his way back from the battle of Largs in 1263.

At the southern end of Kerrera is Gylen Castle which was built in 1582 by the Clan M^{ac}Dougall and razed in 1647 by the Covenanters lead by General Leslie during the Wars of the Three Kingdoms. All the M^{ac}Dougalls were massacred.

Free Night 58

The Covenanters were a Protestant anti-papist movement in the 17th century who had come together in a solemn promise to uphold the Presbyterian faith and loyalty to the King and to oppose the Roman Catholic Church's attempts to regain any foothold or authority in Scotland.

The Big Picture

It's the essence of science to weigh, measure and look,
To know the smallest details, record them in our books.
We have to take to pieces, reduce to smallest part,
Dismantle, disassemble, get right into the heart.

And as we see specifics, with learnèd eyes so wise,
Our narrowed field of vision observeth not the prize.
For what we seek to fathom, is not in details found,
It's in the panorama, just take a look around!

Reducing all to numbers, statistics and damn lies,
We fail to learn true value, and merely know the price.
So lift your gaze t'ward heaven, let nature be your guide,
Instructed by creation, behold! The earth and sky.

Andrew Dalby, Horseshoe Bay, Kerrera, 18th June 2013.

"That haughtiness which goes with knowledge and feeling,
which shrouds the eyes and senses of man in a blinding
fog, therefore deceives him about the value
of existence by carrying in itself the most
flattering evaluation of knowledge itself.
Its most universal effect is
deception; ..." [22]
Nietzsche

"Intelligence means the ability to handle knowledge
as a whole; this is what humans excelled
at in prehistory. It is we who are
cognitively undeveloped." [23]
John Zerzan

This poem arose out my sense of place during our time by
Kerrera. When we stop to look at our surroundings, (I mean
properly look that involves seeing and noticing) it is amazing
what there is to see. Often in life we are so tied up with the
next thing we must do that we develop a sort of tunnel vision.
If we step back for a moment and raise our gaze, the grandeur
and magnificence of creation stands over and around us and,
if you will let it, a sense of wonder grows that makes us feel
alive again.

-oOo-

Monday 24th June 2013, Port Ramsay Lismore, N4-5 Cloudy,
Baro 1024, Day 293:
*After two weeks residency off Kerrera we set sail for the
Island of Lismore and we managed to sail quite a large part
of the 11 miles to get here. We have come to the North West
corner of the island and anchored in a very pleasant bay with
2 other yachts. This is Port Ramsay. There are a lot of lime
kilns around here and the village has a row of white cottages*

as well as a few more scattered dwellings, one with a turf roof. There also appears to be a gypsy caravan. I am looking forward to going ashore to investigate.

Free Night 70

Tuesday 25th June 2013, Port Ramsay Lismore, SW3 Overcast, Baro 1028, Day 294:

I went ashore at low tide with the aim of foraging for mussels and other shell fish. I found a few mussels but in such small numbers that it was neither worthwhile nor ethical to pick them. There was plenty of evidence of cockles in the form of empty shells but I could not find them alive in any quantities and the razor clams squirted as I approached, but they were far too deeply buried to be disgorged!

Thwarted in my attempts to become a hunter gatherer I decided to take the dogs ashore for a walk! Having spent quite a while on the east beach I elected to exercise the dogs on the west beach which had me curious on account of the rows of low metal structures which were entirely submerged for half of the tide. On closer inspection it turned out to be an oyster farm! The oysters are grown in mesh bags made from what appears to be lead, or a lead like material, which measure about 18 inches by 2 feet 6 inches (45cm by 75cm) on supporting frames that keep them about 18 inches (45cm) off the sea bed. Leading up off the beach into the sand dunes is a path made of broken oyster shells at the end of which is a shack with a sign on the door saying, "Smokehouse and Packing Shed".

I also saw a heron, 2 ravens and numerous oyster catchers. Given the fact that oysters move more slowly than stones oyster catcher is a name that is hardly an accolade in praise of their athleticism or hunting skills!

Free Night 71

Wednesday 26th June 2013, Port Ramsay, NW3 – W Sunny, Baro 1036, Day 295:

I went ashore today in search of the standpipe water supply mentioned in the pilot book. The village was deserted apart from one elderly gentleman who ignored my "Hello", went indoors and came back out when I had given up in my quest for the standpipe and climbed aboard the dinghy. Initially I forgave him reasoning that his non response may have been due to hearing impairment, but his re-emergence upon my departure left me feeling I was unwelcome. I returned to Drumlin for lunch and returned to the shore later via the oyster beds with Chip. The gypsy caravan turned out to be a beautiful chalet on an eco-campsite and the elusive water pipe is located not in the village, but at the croft house with the turf roof. Whilst at the campsite I met a Dutch couple on holiday from Amsterdam. They were so thrilled by the mountainous Scottish landscape coming as they did from a flat part of the planet. They were in for a treat as the next destination on their itinerary was to be Ullapool, a place I know well from past family holidays.

Free Night 72

Saturday 29th June 2013, Horseshoe Bay Kerrera, S5 Rain, Day 298:

We have begun to run low on provisions, Port Ramsay does not have a shop and there are high winds forecast so we decided to return to Oban. Our original intention was to anchor in the anchorage shown on the charts and pilot books in Ardintrive Bay, but once again we found that it is completely over-run with marina moorings. Horseshoe Bay it is then, again.

Free Night 75

Sunday 30th June 2013, Cardingmill Oban, SSE 5-7/8, Baro 1014, Day 299:

Horseshoe bay is normally quite sheltered, but a south easterly wind has an uninterrupted passage straight up the sound of Kerrera and into the bay and despite being tandem anchored with all our chain out in relatively shallow water, we dragged. Even after resetting the anchor we still could not keep our station, so we gave up and took a mooring here at Oban Sailing Club's Cardingmill moorings. Claire went down with a migraine headache which confined her to bed for the rest of the day. Bracken took on "nursing" duties and lay beside her on <u>my side of the bed!</u> I went ashore and brought back about half of the provisions we need. The supermarket is a long walk and a rucksack full of tins and two shopping bags are all I can manage on foot.

Monday 1st July 2013, Horseshoe Bay Kerrera- Again, S3-4 Broken Cloud and Sun, Baro 1013, Day 300:

Our enforced sojourn in Oban has enabled us to stock up on provisions, do some banking and to discover that the Oban laundry is not self-service and has a long, long waiting time with fees starting at £8.00. I set to with a bucket and an improvised washing line. Drying is the issue, let us hope tomorrow is a drying day! We also became a little extravagant and treated ourselves to fish and chips for lunch. This is a luxury we really miss and periodically have cravings for.

Free night 76

Wednesday 3rd July 2013, Port Ramsey, W3 Fair, Baro 1008, Day 302:

We have returned to Port Ramsay today because we like it here and the forecast is for a period of unsettled weather, so we have squeezed into a tiny anchorage east of Eilean Ramsay and Eilean Droineach, we hope it will be more sheltered in here. We managed a good sail up the Lynn of Lorn covering at least 6 of the 11 miles for free. At last some cheaper travelling using less motor. Once securely anchored, Claire went ashore to render assistance to a ewe which had caught its horns in a wire mesh fence. After a struggle she succeeded in liberating the poor creature which ran off none the worse for its ordeal.

16 kayakers paddled past us this evening.

Free Night 78

Sunday 7th July 2013, Port Ramsay Lismore, S2 Very Sunny, Baro 1036, Day 306:
It has been a glorious day, sufficiently sunny and warm that we have been able to stay in the cockpit from 8.30 this morning until 8.30 this evening, but we did require a sun canopy up. We listened to the radio as Andy Murray won the Wimbledon Men's Singles Championship in 3 straight sets, 6-4, 7-5, 6-4. He is the first British man to win for 77 years! Claire made homemade Scotch pancakes with strawberry jam to celebrate the occasion.

For the first time in 2 weeks we have been able to see the top of Ben Nevis and all the other mountains around us.

Free Night 82

Monday 8th July 2013, Port Ramsay Lismore, 32°C in the shade, Baro 1035, Day 307:
Today has been a very hot and sunny day and we took the opportunity to go for a long walk. There is a Broch on the east side of the island of Lismore about half way down. Brochs are Iron Age secure dwellings about 2000 years old. Originally it would have been about 15 meters high, but now only 4 or 5 meters remain as the stone has been robbed for later buildings in the area. The Tirfuir Broch stands on the

top of a craggy ridge, it would have been a very impressive sight and very safe for its residents. The walk was about 5 miles in total and on our return we had to pass a farm where a sheep dog took it upon herself to walk all the way back to Port Ramsay with us. No amount of encouragement could make her turn back. When we arrived back at the beach we climbed into the dinghy and rowed back to Drumlin; the sheepdog stood and watched looking very disappointed and dejected. We hope she made it home alright!

Free Night 83

Wednesday 10th July 2013, Port Ramsay, Variable 2-3 Sunny, Baro 1027, Day 309:
It is one year today since we embarked upon our adventure. The reality is that it is as hard as we imagined and as rewarding.

I took the dinghy and visited the neighbouring islands Eilean Ramsay and Eilean Droineach. From their west sides they overlook the Lynn of Morvern, a stunningly beautiful landscape marred only by the titanic amputation of the side of the mountain by a super quarry. Matthew chapter 17 verse 20, "Jesus said ... If you have faith as a grain of mustard seed..." Mercifully faith is not a material commodity to be exploited by industry, but I am convinced moving mountains is possible with dynamite and machinery. The damage they are doing to this mountain for the sake of commerce persuades me why God would not entrust mankind with any greater powers to butcher the planet. Even here where remoteness makes procuring drinking water, for example, a logistical consideration, not to mention provisions, one is continually reminded by the drone of the distant machines and the sight of the Earth's open wound just how malignant civilisation is, and how difficult it is to escape from it.

"If a man walk in the woods for love of them half of each
day, he is in danger of being regarded as a loafer;
but if he spends his whole day as a speculator,
shearing off those woods and making earth
bald before her time, he is esteemed an
industrious and enterprising
citizen." [24]
Henry David Thoreau

Thursday 11th July 2013, Oitr Mhor Bay Kerrera, S2-3 Sunny, Baro 1024, Day 310:
We have returned once again to Oban so that we can stock up on provisions and take on water. The weather has been very hot and calm so we have had to use the engine all the way here from Port Ramsay. After making a couple of trips to the supermarket we came to Oitir Mhor Bay (meaning large shoal) on the north western edge of Kerrera and managed to anchor after two attempts due to the chain becoming tangled in the locker. We were entertained this evening by an otter that had caught a fish that looked to be about 4 or 5lb in weight whilst it floated on its back and ate it.

Free Night 86

Sunday 14th July 2013, Horseshoe Bay Kerrera, 19.45 hrs, SW3 Cool with Sunny Spells, Baro 1027, Day 313:
Yesterday the wind picked up and came round to the north west making Oitir Mhor uncomfortable so we have returned to our old haunt Horseshoe Bay, again.

As we are about half way through our first truly nomadic season I thought it might be interesting to look back through our log book and gather some statistics:-

1.   *Since starting our adventure we have had 89 free nights out of 313 aboard, that is about 28%.*
2.   *So far this season we have covered 522NM and the engine has run for about 121 hours. Assuming that on average we motor at about 3.5 knots we have motored 423NM and, therefore only sailed a mere 99 NM. A lousy 19% spent under sail.*
3.   *Since we left Troon we have been at sea 102 days, 28 days had rain, 44 days had some sunshine, 21 days had winds in excess of F6 and 4 days had thick fog. Often some of these were in combination on the same day.*

We are hoping to set sail for Tobermory tomorrow.

Free Night 89

Monday 15th July 2013, Loch Aline, SW3-4 Rain, Baro 1025, Day 314:

We left Horseshoe Bay this morning and hoisted the main sail as soon as the anchor was up and we managed to sail as far as Craignure before the wind dropped and we had to motor the rest of the way. There is quite a strong current that runs through the Sound of Mull.

Loch Aline is a very sheltered sea loch with a strong tidal stream through its narrow entrance. It is very beautiful apart from the silica mine. Apparently there are 30 miles of tunnels inside the mountain. The Morvern Peninsular is an isolated place with access by boat much easier than by road. A car ferry runs from Aline village across to Mull where a short trip by road brings you to Craignure and another ferry crossing to Oban. After arriving at our anchorage it started to rain heavily, the first rain we have had in a few weeks.

Free Night 90

Wednesday 17th July 2013, Tobermory, SSW3-4 Overcast, Baro 1012, Day 316:

On departing Loch Aline this morning we saw another Otter and once into the Sound of Mull we beat our way westwards and then as our course turned north west we managed to sail close hauled right up to Tobermory. 10 good miles under sail!

In Tobermory we anchored close in by the pontoons. An old music pupil of mine had moved to Calgary on Mull a few years ago and I decided to try to contact him. As luck would have it he was actually in Tobermory for the evening at the sailing club so I spent a pleasant evening watching him sailing with his friends while talking to his Mum.

Free night 92

Thursday 18th July 2013, Tobermory, Sunny, Baro 1028, Day 317:

We did a little exploring ashore today and took in the sights of Tobermory. Everybody raves about this place and it is a favourite haunt of yachtsmen. I really wanted to hate it, but I have to admit that it is a lovely place. The brightly painted buildings along the sea front are as vivid and vibrant as an illustration in a child's picture book, which indeed they have become in the fictional town of Balamory, but they do seem to sit comfortably in the majestic Scottish landscape like rainbow plumed parrots blend into a rain forest. Add to this scene the evocative sounds of the pipes and drums parading through the streets as part of the Highland Gathering that was being held on the school playing fields above town and you have a piece of authentic Scottish culture, not the saccharin stereotype of porridge oats and shortbread tins, but genuine real island life. In the evening the festivities continued with ceilidhs and live music.

Free Night 93

Friday 19th July 2013, Arinagour Coll, NW3 Fog Patches Sunny, Baro 1029, Day 318:

We motored northwards from Tobermory up the Sound of Mull then sailed into fog at the south end of Ardnamurchan, but it was not too bad. We had a NW3 on the beam so we managed to sail all the way across to the island of Coll. We anchored just south of the village stone pier in clear blue water with a beautiful sandy bottom. All 12 of the visitor moorings filled up since we arrived as well as another 7 boats at anchor. This is a busy little place.

We saw several dolphins today, the first for quite a long time. We also saw a lot of puffins. The north end of Coll appears to be a barren place with thin soil and bare rock, to the south it seems to be flatter with machair and sandy beaches. Arinagour is the main village on the island with most of the island's 150 or so inhabitants living in this area. At the southern seaward end of the loch, loch Eartharna, Calmac have a large R0-Ro ferry terminal.

Drumlin sailed herself very well under full canvas with only the auto helm to guide her for about 10NM. The sea was slight.

Free Night 94

Saturday 20th July 2013, Arinagour Coll, Sunny, Baro 1026, Day 319:

Coll seems to be a much more self-sufficient island than any small island we have visited so far. We put this fact down to the relative infrequency of the ferry service. The people, many of whom are non "Collachs", are very welcoming and friendly and all the facilities a visiting yachtsman may need are available at reasonable cost. Even the moorings were cheaper than most we have encountered so far, £10 on Coll and £15 elsewhere. I find Coll a very charming and beautiful

147

place. If I had a bicycle I would have explored much more of it. The water is crystal clear, so much so that we can actually see our anchor and chain on the sea bed even though it is 6 or 7 meters (18 – 20 feet) to the bottom.

Free Night 95

Sunday 21st July 2013, Gott Bay Skarinish Tiree, S2 Sunny, Baro 1019, Day 320:

We motored south to the northern end of Tiree and it feels like the edge of the world here, not least because it is right on the edge of the charts we are carrying. It is a lovely place, but it does have an atmosphere a little like an army camp. Everything is here, Gigha take note. Tiree has a butcher, a baker and a candlestick maker. Okay, a small supermarket, a butcher who bakes his own pies, so a baker as well, another village shop, a van selling burgers and ice-cream, a bank, and an electrical shop selling white goods! Needs are met on these two islands, not by a twice hourly ferry like Gigha!

We had anchored close to another yacht in Gott Bay which on closer inspection was flying the Norwegian flag. Claire forbade me from hoisting mine or making contact. Kill joy!

Gott Bay is a semicircle and over a mile in diameter. It has beautiful white sandy beaches and the houses are spread thinly and fairly uniformly along the edge. It has a feeling of uncluttered space, wide skies, fairly flat land and broad expanses of water. For some reason it reminds me of Goathland on the North Yorkshire Moors (The fictional village of Aidensfield in the television series Heartbeat) because it is open, green and well garnished in sheep droppings and tufts of wool. Oh, and sheep!

Free Night 96

Monday 22nd July 2013, Got Bay Tiree, E2-3 Sunny, Baro 1013, Day 321:
It has been officially declared as the hottest day in the UK since 2006. It was also announced today that her Royal Highness The Duchess of Cambridge Countess of Strathearn and Lady Carrickfergus, Princess Catherine to most of us, has gone into labour. We await the birth of the 43rd monarch and 3rd in line to the throne with interest.

We walked the dogs on the big white sandy beach. Later on I went into the village to buy some bread and salad and on the way back to the bay I was kindly given a lift back to the dinghy by the local policeman's wife. I think she perhaps remembered me from yesterday's dog walk when we passed her house in the evening. Her husband is the only police constable on both Coll and Tiree, which over the past couple of days has been hosting a music festival for which he had a few colleagues brought in. Because there are so many people visiting the island for the festival, Calmac have put on an extra ferry, but even that was not enough to take everyone off the island who wanted to go. Some had to be left behind, stranded like a herd of Robinson Crusoes. There are worse islands to be stranded on!

20.30 hrs - ITS A BOY! Prince George Alexander according to BBC Radio 4.
Free Night 97

Tuesday 23rd July 2013, Sailean Mor Oronsay Loch Sunart, S3> Thunder and Lightening Torrential Rain, Baro 1010, Day 322:
We set sail northwards from Tiree and enjoyed a fair wind for a few hours before we heard the ominous rumbling of thunder to the south east. The storm eventually struck directly above us as we were passing the entrance to Loch Eartharna on Coll

which leads into Arinagour village. Coll has few trees. In fact the tallest object for as far as the eye could see was Drumlin's mast which is made of metal and therefore a good conductor of electricity. We felt vulnerable, so much so that we draped a length of anchor chain around the base of the mast and lead it over the port side into the water to act as a lightening conductor. We noticed that all the birds, most of them puffins, had settled on the sea and nothing was flying around us. The nearest lightening strike was less than a mile away. After the storm abated the air was still, as if petrified by the terror and fury of the weather, so we motored the rest of the way to Oronsay, a small island in Loch Sunart just north of Tobermory. Sailean Mor is a tiny inlet on the northern side of the island with a tight entrance. It is very sheltered. When we were snugly settled in we were greeted by a common seal and her cub suckling on a nearby rock.

Free Night 98

Chapter Eight

Retracing Our Steps

"Hansel took his little sister by the hand, and
followed the pebbles which shone like
newly-coined silver pieces, and
showed them the way."
Hansel and Gretel
Brothers Grimm

Friday 26th July 2013, Tobermory, Variable 2 Sunny, Baro
1009, Day 325:
*After a quiet and relaxing couple of days on Oronsay we
returned to Tobermory after lunch this afternoon managing to
sail for most of the way albeit at a pedestrian 2.5 knots. Once
reinstalled in the anchorage almost exactly where we had
been before, we went ashore with the dogs. Tobermory was
bustling and busy, not with the levity and merrymaking of the
party atmosphere previously, but with a more businesslike
and sober dignity of a town about its daily chores.*

*Nick, Claire's brother rang and asked if we could meet up
next week to come sailing. We arranged to meet him in Oban
on Monday.*

Free Night 101

Monday 29th July 2013, Oban Sailing Club, W3-5 Sunshine
and Showers, Baro 1000, Day 328:
*We have returned to Oban and Nick and his son Matthew
have joined us aboard Drumlin for a few days. This morning
another Nick and Jill, sailing friends of ours from Yorkshire,*

visited us as they were in the area on their yacht "Amadea".
This afternoon we visited the supermarket for provisions.

Tuesday 30th July 2013, Port Ramsay, SW3-5 Sunshine and
Showers, Baro 1006, Day 329:
Given that we had spent so many happy days anchored in
Port Ramsay we thought it would be a good place to take Nick
and Matthew for a mini cruise. We sailed about 8 of the 10 or
so miles it is from Oban to Port Ramsay and when we arrived
I took Matthew, our 15 year old nephew ashore in the dinghy
to explore.

Free Night 104

Wednesday 31st July 2013, Horseshoe Bay, SE2-3 Fair, Baro
1009, Day 330:
We sailed back from Lismore to Oban to return our guests to
shore passing Amadea and her crew, Nick and Jill, heading
the opposite way back to Loch Creran. We drew alongside for
a quick exchange of pleasantries before pressing on to our
respective destinations. Having set Nicholas and Matthew
down in Oban we returned to what now almost seems to be
our second home, Horseshoe Bay!

Free Night 105

For the next few days we were unable to continue our journey
back to the Clyde as we had planned owing to fairly brisk
winds to near gales from the south, so we have had to remain
patient and static. Finally our opportunity seemed to came on
the 5th August, but my serenity was tested to the limits again
by the day's frustrations and aggravations.

Monday 5th August 2013, Ardinamir Bay Torsa, WSW2-3
Showers, Baro 1009, Day 335:
Having waited until today to come south we need not have
bothered. The forecast north westerly that promised a steady

broad reach down the Firth of Lorn to Luing turned out to be a south westerly putting the wind almost on the nose. We didn't set off yesterday because of the south westerlies and have wasted a day of our lives waiting for favourable winds that did not materialise. At least if we had left yesterday we would have had sunshine!

There is a narrow, very narrow, sound that is a short cut from the Firth of Lorn into Loch Melfort avoiding the strong tidal races of the Sound of Luing. It is called Cuan Sound and is a short dog legged white knuckle ride that runs at about 7 knots towards a reef that has to be chicaned having run the gauntlet of the two ferries which ply their way in a scissor action between Seil Island and Luing. It is the nearest I ever want to come to white water rafting in Drumlin! Claire said she enjoyed it...

Once we were safely through Cuan Sound we headed clockwise around Torsa Island and into Ardinamir Bay which is entered via a rock strewn series of twists and turns. It was worth the effort, this is a lovely place.

Free Night 110

Tuesday 6th August 2013, Ardinamir Bay, SE2 Showers, Baro 1013, Day 336:
We walked across the island to Cullipool which is a pretty little community consisting of white painted cottages looking westwards across the Sound of Luing. The cottages, once the homes of slate workers are well kept, and the slate quarries around the village are impressively deep and now full of water. There are a lot of wild flowers and the locals are very friendly. The village shop and post office was well stocked with goods and we managed to buy what we needed.

Today would have been my Mum's 74th Birthday.

Free Night 111

Thursday 8th August 2013, Melfort Pier, 20.15 hrs, S3 Sunshine and Showers, Baro 1013, Day 338:

We sailed the 5 or so miles from Ardinamir anchorage to Melfort and we have settled just off the pier and outside the "harbour". It seems that the pier belongs to a private community of privately owned holiday homes on the Melfort estate. It is made quite clear that this is a private place. All the pilot books indicate that anchoring here is accepted, so we are staying put! The pilot books also say it is a relatively short mile and a quarter walk to the village shop and post office, but after a good mile and a half we turned around. It certainly is a mile and a quarter to the shop, but only if you set off from the right place! Shortly we came upon a local man who said that we had been very nearly where we wanted to be and that another 5 minutes would have seen us there.

Free Night 113

Saturday 10th August 2013, Melfort Pier, SW3-4 Showers, Baro 1019, Day 340:

We have been subjected to heavy showers on and off all day today. This afternoon we gave in to laziness and decided to go shopping in the boat. We motored down the shore to the village where we had walked a few days before and anchored in the bay (Loch na Cille) inside all the local marina's moorings which predictably were crowding out the best places to anchor. I remained aboard Drumlin as we had to use a short scope of chain and we were not convinced how well she would hold, and Claire rowed ashore. She did indeed find the shop just a short distance beyond where we had previously turned around. Happily the shop carried a wide range of items and we provisioned the boat with enough to see us through the next week. We pottered back to Melfort Pier again where we spent the rest of the day celebrating our 28th wedding anniversary.

Free Night 115

Private, No Fishing!

It's private, no fishing here.
It's only for the toffs,
So sling your hook, don't push your luck,
Or risk the Gillie's wrath.

The river's bounty along its length
Is only for the few.
The ones with money, power and strength,
Not common men, like you.

It's private, no fishing here,
These facts you here must face,
Obey the rules or live in fear,
And peasant, know thy place.

It's private, no fishing here,
What does this really say?
It says, "You cross the line
If you cast a line,
At any time for,
These fish are mine.
It's private, no fishing here!"

Yet, what Nature yields she gives to all,
To rich and poor, to great and small,
No distinction does she make,
'Twixt man or beast for goodness sake.

What right the rich to hoard it all,
To deny the poor man leave
Who could but nearly feed himself,
If allowed to fish for free?

It's private, no fishing here,
These facts you here must face,
It's the ones with money, power and strength,
Not peasants! Know thy place.

That little sign, on river banks
Proclaims injustice clear,
That inequality ever reigns.
It's private, no fishing here.

Andrew Dalby, Loch Melfort, 10th August 2013

This poem was inspired by a shore visit to Melfort. As I walked along the road beside the river I saw the 'No Fishing' signs and the river also appeared to be overtly garrisoned behind my favourite symbol of division, inequality and oppression, the fence. I grew up fishing the becks and rivers of North Yorkshire as a small boy and this sign "Private, No Fishing" is fairly ubiquitous, but today I saw it differently; for the first time I saw it for what it really is.

-oOo-

Monday 12th August 2013, Craignish Lagoon, W4-5 Sunshine and Showers, Baro 1014, Day 342:
We needed to arrive at the Dorus Mor narrows in time to catch a favourable east flowing tide in order to get into loch Craignish and this meant a relatively early start. We weighed anchor at 8am and made 5 to 6 knots under full sail. What is even more satisfying is the fact that the firm and steady westerly blow was perfect for the reach southwards towards the left turn we had to make to pass east through the narrow channel that is the Dorus Mor. Being a naturally cautious man I started the engine as we approached the tidal race, but I resolutely refused to put her in gear as we were swept like a leaf down a storm drain through

the venturi between Craignish Point and Garbh Reisa at over 9 knots. That was fun!

Free Night 117

Wednesday 14th August 2013, Craignish Lagoon, SE4-5 Sunshine and Showers, Baro 1015, Day 344:

It would have been Neil's 22nd birthday today; our daughter Hannah telephoned to say that she and some friends had been to his grave in the village church yard and put some flowers on. We spent the day quietly reading and I studied the charts and pilot books in preparation for our trip around the Mull of Kintyre.

Free Night 119

Thursday 22nd August 2013, Ardminish Bay Gigha, S – Variable 3 Fair, Baro 1015, Day 352:

We left the Lagoon at 2.30pm and made our way to the marina at Ardfern where we replenished the jerry can with diesel and topped up the water tank. By 4pm we were ready to set off to Gigha with a favourable tide. The first 6 miles were a beautiful sail, but then the wind dropped necessitating the use of the engine for the remaining 25 miles. We arrived at Gigha at half past midnight in complete darkness and anchored inside the moorings assisted by our torch and a bright full moon, the only sign of welcome, as the port hand marker buoy indicating the extremity of the reef across the entrance to the bay was extinguished. A nerve wracking approach knowing that behind the warm black velvet cloak of darkness are numerous treacherous lumps of rock laying in wait for any unsuspecting, gung-ho mariner.

Free Night 127

Saturday 24th August 2013, Campbeltown, W2-3 Fair, Baro 1014, Day 354:

At 7am this morning we struck out of Ardminish Bay bound for the Mull of Kintyre and Campbeltown. As we passed the southern end of Gigha, the island no longer acting as a breakwater, the sea developed a big rolling westerly swell lurching across our beam, and it steadily increased as we headed further south. By the time we had reached Macrihanish Bay things were becoming quite rough and I feared an unwelcome reunion with my breakfast. As we were rounding the western corner of the Mull the tide had not quite turned to our advantage making the overfalls pitch and toss Drumlin like a child's toy in a bath. Soon we had turned east and the mighty hand of the tide smoothed our way leaving my morning repast to continue its own journey with no further threat of diversion. Soon we could see the Sound of Sanda opening out and the sea was calm and the wind at our back. We sailed through and continued northward to Campbeltown Loch where we returned to the scene of our earlier anchoring faux pas, but this time we avoided becoming entangled in the remains of HMS Breda.

As has become my almost daily ritual I cast my hand line over the side not expecting to catch anything. Why would I? In five months of performing this same rite I have had not so much as a nibble, not even when fish have obviously been gathered around the boat mocking and jeering me for my ineptitude. But not tonight! Finally I was able to hold my hunter gather head up high and echo the words of my friend Cameron, "Am no stoopit!" and landed not 1, not 2 but 6 mackerel. The dogs had never seen such mayhem and chaos, and could not help celebrating my success by getting in the way to investigate these strange silver shining, wriggling, salty and smelly things. Order restored I put two fish back (taking only what is needed) and we enjoyed our second free meal of the trip!

Free Night 129

Sunday 25th August 2013, Campbeltown, NW3 Sunny, Baro 1018, Day 355:

It has been a day of beautiful warm sunshine. We rowed ashore and walked with the dogs into town passing the Commonwealth War Cemetery and a children's play park along the mile or so of promenade to the smart and fairly recently renovated town waterfront. This was the first time Claire had been into the town since the year 2000 and she was favourably impressed by the improvements and obvious investment that has taken place. On a similar singlehanded visit I had made in 2003 when sailing our previous boat "Rachel", I read an advert in a local shop window inviting musicians to come along and enjoy rehearsals with the Campbeltown Brass Band. I'd have loved to, being a brass musician myself, but the poster did not say where or when rehearsals were held! I mention this because today the Campbeltown Band was playing at an open air church service at the harbour and we stayed to listen.

Free Night 130

Thursday 29th August 2013, Kingscross Point Lamlash Bay, W2-3, Baro 1018, Day 359:

As soon as we had the anchor onboard we were able to hoist the sails and waft out of Campbeltown Loch at a majestic 2.5 knots and we persevered under canvass to within about a mile of Pladda, a small island with an impressive light house just off the south coast of the Isle of Arran where the tidal stream became a little too overpowering, so we motored until clear of it. Having broken free of the current I was determined to make the best use of the light air and set full sail again for the few remaining miles north to Lamlash Bay. This is a decision I am glad I made because our quiet serenity a little way south of Holy Island persuaded an approaching 8 metre cetorhinus maximus, the world's second largest fish to continue feeding in her nonchalant zigzag manner, and not to descend and hide in the depths. She continued thus until within a boat's length of our bow whereupon she calmly curtsied past almost within touching distance of our starboard side and continued on her way. Had we not been aware of the possibility of seeing such creatures and having learnt that they are entirely benign plankton – eating animals, our first close encounter with a basking shark may have been more terrifying than exhilarating. This was a truly "Wow" moment.

Free Night 134

Saturday 31st August 2013, Kingscross Point, W4-6 Sunshine and Showers, Baro 1027, Day 361:
About 40 yachts of all shapes and sizes sailed into the north entrance of Lamlash and out of the south end today. It was clearly a race and very entertaining too.

Free Night 136

Wednesday 4th September 2013, Kingscross Point, SE2-3 Sunshine and Clouds, Baro 1015, Day 365:
It is our 365th day aboard, a year of life afloat although it is actually more than a year since we embarked upon this adventure as we do not count days spent away from Drumlin.

We have been loafing around in Lamlash killing time waiting to return to Troon as we are going to visit Claire's parents. They are celebrating their 50th wedding anniversary and all the family will be there. We plan to return to Troon tomorrow to prepare for the trip and to make space for my father's sojourn with us next week. In the mean time we have been reading, watching the Lamlash inshore lifeboat doing exercises with an Air Sea Rescue helicopter and I deflated the dinghy and put it away on the foredeck.

Free Night 140

-oOo-

Monday 9th September 2013, Troon, Sunshine and Showers, Baro 1020, Day 369:

I returned the hire car to Irvine and bought an adaptor for the gas bottle connector from a local caravan and camping company which means we can now use any size of gas bottle, not just the smallest 4.5kg ones we have been confined to so far. We will now be able to make a saving through the economies of scale as the bigger bottles are proportionately cheaper for the amount of gas they hold, and we can manage to carry a 15kg bottle with ease. My father Malcolm arrived with us today and we went out to a local restaurant for a meal. It is a year to the day that my Mum died, tomorrow it is a year to the date.

Tuesday 10th September 2013, Troon, NW5-6 Sunny, Baro 1023, Day 370:

Today has been a day with a degree of melancholy, but we spent the time making rehearsal CDs for a musical that Malcolm has arranged for the Filey Salvation Army. We are planning on going for a little cruise tomorrow as the wind and weather look promising.

Wednesday 11th September 2013, Millport Great Cumbrae, Rain Showers, Baro 1021, Day 371:

The day began very wet in Troon but after lunch the rain stopped so we set off for Millport. The wind dropped as we were passing Ardrossan so we motored for the second part of the journey. We picked up one of Scotland's few remaining free at the point of use, one time Highland and Islands Enterprise mooring buoys. We were serenaded by seals "singing" at dusk!

Free Night 141

Thursday 12th September 2013, Tarbert Loch Fyne, W5-6 Rain, Baro 1014, Day 372:

We enjoyed a peaceful and quiet night in Millport and we made our way to Tarbert Via the bottom end of the Island of Bute. As is usual this area of sea is prone to swell and we enjoyed the customary "bounce" that characterises all passages through these waters. We sailed very successfully across Inchmarnock to the Cowal Peninsular when the wind dropped and we again resorted to the engine. At times the rain made visibility poor and to be honest the weather was rather worse than we had anticipated. It is a shame that a late summer cruise for Malcolm turned out to be such an uncomfortable drudge, but we were all rewarded with two sightings of basking sharks and a safe arrival in Tarbert. Later in the evening we took a stroll around the town and on arriving back in harbour found "Lemara", a beautifully kept gentleman's motor launch that is owned by a friend of Malcolm's from Filey. It was late, so we shall pay a surprise call on them in the morning.

Friday 13th September 2013, Troon, NW3 Sunshine, Baro 1020, Day 373:

The day began with Malcolm and I sauntering round to Lemara's berth and knocking on the door to surprise the owner, another Malcolm, and his wife. We spent a lovely hour or so marvelling at the workmanship of this beautiful boat and learning from Malcolm some of the tricks of the trade necessary to keep such a vessel in this sort of superlative condition. It boils down to three things; patience, persistence and hard work!

At lunch time we headed off for home and with a steady north westerly behind us we managed to goose-wing Drumlin for 20 miles at a respectable 4 knots. Remarkably, having only ever once encountered a basking shark before this year, today we sighted another near Bute which brings our total to four this year.

Finally, as is the way of things at this time of day, the wind dropped again and we had to motor the final few miles to Troon.

Chapter Nine

Coda

"Those things which I am saying now
may be obscure, yet they will be
made clearer in their
proper place." [25]
Nicolaus Copernicus

We have achieved what we set out to do. We have sold our home, bought a boat, set up a property business and sailed off on a voyage of discovery. Now it is the end of our first full season of cruising and hopefully the first of many more to come. Who knows? The future is uncertain. That is a lesson we learnt long ago with Neil. What we have also learnt is that life is for living, whatever that means to us as individuals. This way of life is not for everyone, but living life, my life, your life, is about what the ancient Greeks called "arête", a word which has unfortunately been translated into English many times as *virtue*, a word carrying a completely different idea to the one intended by the Greek. This word has another more subtle side to its definition which can perhaps be summed up as *being the best you can be*. Sometimes being the best we can be means we have to be honest with ourselves and ask the question, "Who am I trying to please?" I spent many decades trying to please other people, to live up to their expectations, to live according to their rules, and it did not work. I changed the game, I changed the rules and now I live my own life. I am happier, less stressed and I have more time for the things that matter.

Know Your Enemy.

Know your enemy. That's the trick.
If you know him, you can win.
But if you're fighting with yourself,
The outcome could be grim!

Know your enemy. There's a thought.
You might even learn to like him,
So if you're fighting with yourself,
It's time to throw the towel in.

Know your enemy. Here's the deal…
To make this conflict end
Stop this fighting with yourself,
And with yourself be friends!

Andrew Dalby, Thirsk, 19th July 2009

Medication is not always the most appropriate response to depression. I have tried it many times and was never cured. For this reason I concluded that there must be another way.

"But the worst enemy you can encounter will
always be you, yourself; you lie in wait
for yourself in caves and woods." [26]
Nietzsche

-oOo-

A number of years ago I discovered the ideas of the Greek Philosopher Antisthenes (c. 445–365 BCE), who was the founder of cynicism, not the popular modern misconception of the word, but the ancient philosophical movement. From his teachings, as I understand them, I have formed my own model for life and I share it here for what it is worth.

The goal of life is to be happy and this is achieved by being the best we can be (arête). To do this requires a positive mental attitude along with five other key qualities:
1. Minimalism; it is important to keep things as simple as possible.
2. Unashamed; it is vital to banish the most damaging emotion of all which is guilt and shame. We must move on from the wrong we have done, from the things that haunt us, and we must not be afraid that our life is not what others expect. We must forgive ourselves! Never be afraid to be yourself and be true to yourself. Be unashamed!
3. Self-reliant; we need to cultivate independence. We live in a world that continually tries to ensnare us. Debt is the most obvious. This is a good thing from the point of view of "The System". An indebted person is more controllable and predictable and profitable! Just like a cow, an imprisoned machine existing for the sole purpose of profiting the farmer until it is of no further use! By being more self-reliant we gradually release ourselves from the talons of servitude.
4. In tune with nature; being natural, living naturally we will thrive better. Consider the battery hen and the eagle. Which would you rather be? It's easy for a battery hen, she is housed, fed and worked to death. That is not natural, neither is the way humans live in the 21st century.

5.   Critical thinking; not critical in a hostile way to criticise and complain about others, but to question why things are the way they are, to identify what is behind the motives of others and to establish what is in one's own best interest.

Predictably for me, and you may have already noticed from the list above, I have reduced this to a simple mnemonic, which by a happy coincidence for a musician like myself, is MUSIC! Here is my philosophy for life:

Try to be the best you can be through the positive pursuit of MUSIC!

Love Thyself as Thy Neighbour!

That's it then!
It's either you or me.
But when I was a child I learned,
Put others first, you see.

But the point they never made
When driving home this lesson,
To love thy neighbour as thyself,
Not more! No self repression.

So if I love myself a lot
And treat myself so kind,
I'll treat you others just as well,
I'm sure that you won't mind!

Andrew Dalby, Thirsk, 22nd July 2009

"For one thing is needful: that a human
being attain his satisfaction
with himself-" [27]
Nietzsche

"Do love thy neighbour as yourself,
but first be such as love
themselves-" [28]
Nietzsche

Better For Us Both.

I don't want to hurt you.
I just can't help it!
If I do what I want
With you it might not fit.

If I do what you want
And not what's suiting me,
Then I get resentful.
A Problem! Don't you see?

And when my mind's in conflict
About whom I'm going to hurt,
I tend to choose to please you,
So I wear my horse hair shirt!

The turmoil that I feel within
Leads to self suppression,
I cannot bear to assert myself,
And this leads to depression.

So to save myself I must be cruel
And care some less for others,
And in so doing function better

167

More able to serve my brothers.

So if I seem a little off
Or somewhat rather selfish,
I need some space to free my mind
My batteries to replenish.

And if I seem a bit on edge,
Or seem to you uncaring,
I need some room to express myself,
And re-adjust my bearing.

Andrew Dalby, Thirsk, 22nd July 2009

It is worth a thought or two about what I have learnt from this experience so far, and I suppose I can sum it up simply by saying the philosophy of keeping things as simple as possible and reducing to the smallest amount possible anything that clutters life is important; emotional clutter as well as the physical. Once we have shuffled off the burdens we carry and start to be more independent and in tune with what is right for us, we find we have more room for manoeuvre. It takes time, it is not easy, but it is liberating and worth the effort. Someone once said, "You can't take it with you!" That is so true...

As far as our finances are concerned, we have found that it is possible to live with less money and have to some degree succeeded, but this required a change of mindset. Our greatest limitation has been not having a fridge or freezer aboard Drumlin and finding ways to overcome this has been challenging. Today people take fresh food for granted because it can be stored for longer and obtained easily. Our new life has made both of these conveniences harder to achieve. To address this problem I asked myself one simple question,

"What would Grandma have done?" In days gone by food that would quickly perish was made at the time it was needed from storable ingredients. Simple staples such as flour, sugar, margarine and eggs can soon be turned into cakes, pancakes, scones and pastry. Fresh vegetables, pickles and preserves add colour and flavour to meals, and of course some tinned foods are necessary in our circumstances. Simplifying the weekly shop has made it cheaper, perhaps healthier and certainly less difficult to procure what we require. All it has taken is the resolve to cook differently. However, the one major change that we have made is this: we now rarely eat meat. This is because of both the cost of it and the fact we cannot store it. The consequence of this has been remarkable in that I have lost all of my excess weight without any effort whatsoever. This coupled with the exercise I now take by being required to walk where once I might have driven has made me half the man I used to be! I am probably now more lean, healthier and happier than I have been since I was a teenager.

I sometimes wonder where my life might have taken me had it not been for the dreadful catastrophe of Neil's illness and the delightful blessing of his life. I am certain of this; it would not have brought me here. I shall be forever grateful that Neil entered the cave of my existence and prodded awake the sleeping bear of my life's potential causing it to emerge blinking and dazed into the daylight of a wilderness full of fun, adventure and fulfilment, instead of dozing it away in the dormitory of futile domestication which is the workhouse we call society.

Nowt!

I came wi' nowt,
I'll go wi' nowt.

When I were born, I knew nowt,
I wore nowt and I owned nowt!

I spend all my life learnin', earnin', yearnin',
Rivin' even thrivin'!
For what?

Nowt!

Didn't bring out wi' me,
Can't tek owt wi' me!

When I'm dead I won't know owt,
Wear owt or own owt!

So …

If came wi' nowt
And I'll go wi' nowt,
What 'ave I got to worry about?

Nowt!

Andrew Dalby, Thirsk, 10th August 2009

-oOo-

The Next Beginning!

170

Bibliography

Preface
[1]   Henry David Thoreau, Walden and Other Writings.
Bantam Books, New York, 1962. Edited Krutch J W.
Pg 66

Chapter 1
[2]   Henry David Thoreau, Walden and Other Writings.
Bantam Books, New York, 1962. Edited Krutch J W.
Pg 88

[3]   Nietzsche F, The Portable Nietzsche. New York,
Viking Penguin Inc. 1982. Edited and Translated by
Kaufmann   W. Pg 129

[4]   Henry David Thoreau, Walden and Other Writings.
Bantam Books, New York, 1962. Edited Krutch J
W. Pg 135

[5]   Nietzsche F, The Portable Nietzsche. New York,
Viking Penguin Inc. 1982. Edited and Translated by
Kaufmann   W. Pg 137

[6]   Nietzsche F, The Portable Nietzsche. New York,
Viking Penguin Inc. 1982. Edited and Translated by
Kaufmann   W. Pg 163

[7]   The Bible, Matthew Chapter 6 Verse 19. KJV.

[8]   Henry David Thoreau, Walden and Other Writings.
        Bantam Books, New York, 1962. Edited Krutch J
        W. Pg 372

[9]   Ralph Waldo Emerson, SELF-RELIANCE and Other
        Essays. New York: Dover Publications, Inc. 1993.
        Editor: Stanley Appelbaum. Pgs 28-9

[10]   Kenneth Grahame, The Wind in the Willows.
        www.onlineliterature.com/grahame/windwillows/1/
        Chapter 1 The River Bank

[11]   Henry David Thoreau, Walden and Other Writings.
        Bantam Books, New York, 1962. Edited Krutch J W.
        Pg 172

Chapter 2

[12]   Henry David Thoreau, Walden and Other Writings.
        Bantam Books, New York, 1962. Edited Krutch J W.
        Pg182

Chapter 3

No quotations.

Chapter 4

[13]   Henry David Thoreau, Walden and Other Writings. Bantam Books, New York, 1962. Edited Krutch J W. Pg 82

[14]   Henry David Thoreau, Walden and Other Writings. Bantam Books, New York, 1962. Edited Krutch J W. Pg 359

[15]   Nietzsche F, The Portable Nietzsche. New York, Viking Penguin Inc. 1982. Edited and Translated by Kaufmann   W. Pg 161

[16]   Nietzsche F, The Portable Nietzsche. New York, Viking Penguin Inc. 1982. Edited and Translated by Kaufmann   W. Pg 125

[17]   John Zerzan, Future Primitive Revisited. Port Townsend: Feral House, 2012. Pg 97

Chapter 5

[18]   Ralph Waldo Emerson, SELF-RELIANCE and Other Essays. New York: Dover Publications, Inc. 1993. Editor: Stanley Appelbaum. Pg 73

Chapter 6

[19]   Ralph Waldo Emerson, SELF-RELIANCE and Other Essays. New York: Dover Publications, Inc. 1993. Editor: Stanley Appelbaum. Pg 31

[20]   Ian Mitchell, Isles Of The West. Edinburgh, Birlinn Limited, 2004 Pg 224

[21]   Ralph Waldo Emerson, SELF-RELIANCE and Other Essays. New York: Dover Publications, Inc. 1993. Editor: Stanley Appelbaum. Pg 23

Chapter 7

[22]   Nietzsche F, The Portable Nietzsche. New York, Viking Penguin Inc. 1982. Edited and Translated by Kaufmann   W. Pg 43

[23]   John Zerzan, Future Primitive Revisited. Port Townsend: Feral House, 2012. Pg 116

[24]   Henry David Thoreau, Walden and Other Writings. Bantam Books, New York, 1962. Edited Krutch J W. Pg 369

Chapter 8

No Quotations

Chapter 9

[25]   Nicolaus Copernicus

www.brainyquote.com/citation/quotes/zquotes/n/nic

olausco238365.html#Rsf2tfkRVopUvKRx.99

[26]   Nietzsche F, The Portable Nietzsche. New York, Viking Penguin Inc. 1982. Edited and Translated by Kaufmann   W. Pg 176

[27]   Nietzsche F, The Portable Nietzsche. New York, Viking Penguin Inc. 1982. Edited and Translated by Kaufmann W. Pg 99

[28]   Nietzsche F, The Portable Nietzsche. New York, Viking Penguin Inc. 1982. Edited and Translated by Kaufmann W.   Pg 284

[6]   Nietzsche F, The Portable Nietzsche. New York, Viking Penguin Inc. 1982. Edited and Translated by Kaufmann W.   Pg 163

Acknowledgements

I would like to acknowledge my gratitude to the following authors and publishers for the information provided in their books and resources which, although they have not been directly quoted, have provided useful background information and facts that have been included in this journal.

Peter Moir and Ian Crawford, Argyll Shipwrecks. Wemyss Bay, Moir Crawford, 2003.

Hamish Haswell-Smith, The Scottish Islands A Comprehensive Guide to Every Island. Edinburgh, Canongate Books, 1999.

Anna Ritchie, Viking Scotland. London, B T Batsford Ltd, 1996.

Emerson R W, Nature. London, Penguin Books, 1985

Royal Commission on the Ancient and Historical Monuments of Scotland www.rcahms.gov.uk

CalMac Ferries Ltd.
http://www.calmac.co.uk/corporate-calmac/company-history.htm

Wikipedia, the free encyclopaedia http://en.wikipedia.org

Index of Poems

12831804R00100

Printed in Great Britain
by Amazon